C000172581

Britain's Railways

Rail Atlas
1970

Ian Allan

PUBLISHING

CONTENTS

Front cover: Class 47 No D1529 heads a West Country express on the down main line through Twyford. By 1970 maroon coaching stock on a main line train was rare on the Western Region. R. R. Smith

Rear cover, top: 10-year old Class 31 No 5650 looks to be in need of attention from the painters. It is seen standing alongside the much-lamented Kings Cross signalbox, after being released from its incoming service. B. Bennett

Rear cover, bottom: By 1970, retrenchment had taken its toll on the railway's infrastructure. Here a Class 17 'Clayton' diesel, new only a few years before, ekes out its final days on mineral empties, the entire class being withdrawn by the following year. The station has also seen better days, the seat no longer having the protection of station buildings and a canopy. Lawrie Bowles

First published 2003

ISBN 0 7110 2965 2

All rights reserved. No part of this book may be reproduced or transmitted in any form or by any means, electronic or mechanical, including photocopying, recording or by any information storage and retrieval system, without permission from the Publisher in writing.

© Ian Allan Publishing 2003

Cartography by Map Creation Ltd, Maidenhead

Published by Ian Allan Publishing

an imprint of Ian Allan Publishing Ltd, Hersham, Surrey KT12 4RG.

Printed by Ian Allan Printing Ltd, Hersham, Surrey KT12 4RG.

Code: 0308/

INTRODUCTION

This is the latest in Ian Allan Publishing's new series of historical railway atlases and is designed to focus upon the state of the railway industry on 1 May 1970. The date is critical as it is a few days before the timetable change of that year when a number of services were withdrawn.

By 1970 the majority of the closures envisaged in the Beeching Report, as well as a number that weren't, had been completed, although, as is clear from the maps, there were still a significant number of closures to come — most notably in east Lincolnshire as well as the lines to places like Bridport, Ilfracombe and Minehead. During the late 1960s the Labour Government had come to the conclusion that there were lines that merited retention as part of the country's social fabric and this had resulted in the development of the concept of subsidy. Undoubtedly, without this, the railway passenger network in 1970 would have been significantly smaller than that illustrated here and many more towns and cities would have lost their railway connections. Indeed, apart from the lines that subsequently did close, a number of other lines were under threat of imminent withdrawal — such as that between Shipley and Bradford Forster Square — and it is interesting to note with the benefit of hindsight how important these lines have become to the modern railway industry in certain cases.

One of the consequences of the massive reduction in the railway infrastructure in the 1960s was the growth of railway preservation, although it is illuminating to see how few ex-BR lines were operating under private ownership at the date of the atlas. Preservation was to benefit significantly from the time delay between closure and lifting in a number of cases and these routes are indicated in the atlas. Also shown is the stretch from Ashburton to Buckfastleigh, which, under the ownership of the Dart Valley Railway, had seen a limited service but which was destined to be severed as a result of the construction of the main A38(T) west of Exeter. Today, such is the growth in the importance to the economy of the railway heritage industry, that it is almost inconceivable that the new road would not have been designed to accommodate the railway.

In many respects the most striking change for a contemporary readership will be the huge decline in the number of freight terminals and freight-only lines. In 1970, Britain was still a heavily industrialised nation, with large mining and other heavy industries. The gradual loss of mines was a process that had been going on for centuries as a result of the exhaustion of reserves or problems of geology, but there were still scores of mines nationwide, from Somerset in the southwest to Fife in Scotland, that were rail-connected. Likewise, the steel industry was a major provider of freight traffic. Today, the coal industry is but a pale shadow of its former self and much of that which survives is under threat, whilst the number of iron and steel works throughout the country has also dramatically declined. In 1970, Britain was still producing its own domestically mined iron ore, from Westmoreland and Northamptonshire. Again, this is a type of traffic that still travels by rail, but is now all imported.

The development for these maps has involved considerable research in a variety of publications and, while every effort has been made to ensure correctness, there are no doubt errors. As always, the publishers would be grateful for any information to update or correct information given for use in a future second edition.

Key Page

————————————	Western Region passenger
····························	Western Region freight only
————————————	Eastern Region passenger
····························	Eastern Region freight only
————————————	London Midland Region passenger
····························	London Midland Region freight only
————————————	Southern Region passenger
····························	Southern Region freight only
————————————	Scottish Region passenger
····························	Scottish Region freight only
····························	Private freight only
————————————	Preserved in operation
····························	Preserved (planned or proposed)
————————————	Other passenger lines
CANNING TOWN	Passenger station
CANNING TOWN NORTH	Non-passenger location

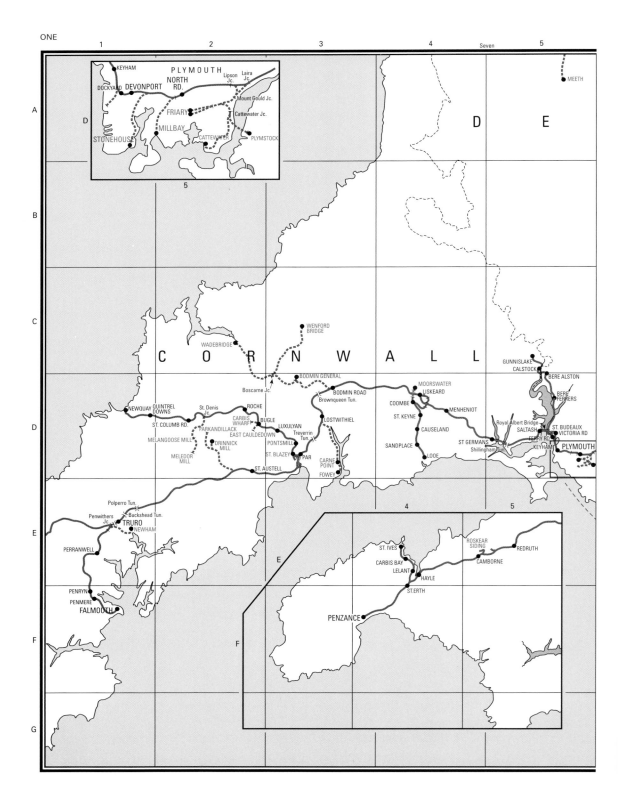

Seven

D

E

PLYMOUTH

KEYHAM
DOCKYARD DEVONPORT NORTH RD.
Lipson Jc. Laira Jc.
Mount Gould Jc.
FRIARY
MILLBAY Cattewater Jc.
STONEHOUSE CATTEWATER
PLYMSTOCK

MEETH

D E

C O R N W A L L

WENFORD BRIDGE

WADEBRIDGE

GUNNISLAKE
CALSTOCK
BERE ALSTON

BODMIN GENERAL
Boscarne Jc.
BODMIN ROAD
Brownqueen Tun.
MOORSWATER
LISKEARD
BERE FERRERS

QUINTREL DOWNS
NEWQUAY
ROCHE
ST. DENIS Jc.
CARBIS WHARF
BUGLE
LUXULYAN
COOMBE
ST. KEYNE
MENHENIOT
ST. COLUMB RD.
EAST CAULDEDOWN
PARKANDILLACK
Treverrin Tun.
LOSTWITHIEL
CAUSELAND
Royal Albert Bridge
SALTASH
ST. BUDEAUX
VICTORIA RD
MELANGOOSE MILL
DRINNICK MILL
PONTSMILL
SANDPLACE
ST GERMANS
FERRY RD.
MELEDOR MILL
ST. BLAZEY
PAR
Shillingham Tun.
KEYHAM
PLYMOUTH
ST. AUSTELL
CARNE POINT
LOOE
FOWEY

Polperro Tun.
Buckshead Tun.
Penwithers Jc.
TRURO
NEWHAM

PERRANWELL

E

ST. IVES
ROSKEAR SIDING
REDRUTH
CARBIS BAY
CAMBORNE
LELANT
PENRYN
HAYLE
PENMERE
ST.ERTH
FALMOUTH

F

PENZANCE

DE**V**ON**S**HIRE

EGGESFORD

LAPFORD

MORCHARD ROAD

COPPLESTONE

TIVERTON JUNC.

HEMYOCK

SAMPFORD COURTENAY

NORTH TAWTON

BOW

YEOFORD

Coleford Jc.

CREDITON

NEWTON ST. CYRES

WHIMPLE

Summit

Honiton Tun.

HONITON

AXMINSTER

Three

OKEHAMPTON

MELDON QUARRY

Yes Tor

Cowley Bridge Jc.

ST. DAVIDS

ST JAMES PARK

Exmouth Jc.

ST. THOMAS

POLSLOE BRIDGE

City Basin Jc.

CENTRAL

EXETER

ALPHINGTON ROAD

TOPSHAM

EXTON

LYMPSTONE

STARCROSS

EXMOUTH

BOVEY

DAWLISH WARREN

DAWLISH

HEATHFIELD

Riviera

TEIGNMOUTH

NEWTON ABBOT

ASHBURTON

Aller Jc.

STONEYCOMBE Summit

Dainton Tun.

Dart Valley Railway

BUCKFASTLEIGH

STAVERTON BRIDGE

TORRE

TORQUAY

Marley Tun.

Totnes (DVR) loop only

Ashburton Jc.

MARSH MILLS

TOTNES

PAIGNTON

GOODRINGTON SANDS

Tavistock Jc.

IVYBRIDGE

Wrangaton Summit

CHURSTON

KINGSWEAR

1 2 3 Eight 4 Nine 5

PORTISHEAD
AVONMOUTH
SHIREHAMPTON
SEA MILLS
FILTON
Westerleigh Junc.
CLIFTON DOWN
BRISTOL
WARMLEY
CHIPPENHAM

W I L T S

TEMPLE MEADS
SEE INSET
St. Annes
Wood Tun.
Brislington Tuns.

A

NAILSEA & BACKWELL
KEYNSHAM & SOMERDALE
SALTFORD
Box Tun.
Thingley Jc.
Middle Hill Tun.

YATTON
Twerton Tun.
WESTON
MIDLAND ROAD
OLDFIELD PARK
MELKSHAM

WESTON MILTON
BATH SPA

Worle Jun.
WESTON - SUPER - MARE
BRADFORD ON AVON
Bradford Jcs.

Uphill Junc.
FRESHFORD
AVONCLIFF
TROWBRIDGE

B

WRITHINGTON
RADSTOCK
WESTBURY

BRENT KNOLL
DILTON MARSH

HIGHBRIDGE
BASON BRIDGE
WHATLEY
FROME

BRIDGWATER
CRANMORE
MEREHEAD
WARMINSTER

C

S O M E R S E T
CASTLE CARY
BRUTON

Castle Cary Junc.
DINTON

Eight
TISBURY

GILLINGHAM

D
Buckhorn Weston Tun.

Summit

PEN MILL

Clifton Maybank Junc.
SHERBORNE
YEOVIL JUNC.
YEOVIL
THORNFORD BRIDGE

YETMINSTER
CREWKERNE
CHETNOLE

CHARD JUNC.
Evershot Tun.

E

D O R S E T
WEST MOORS

WIMBORNE

Two
TOLLER
MAIDEN NEWTON

BRIDPORT
POWERSTOCK
BRANKSOME
BOSCOMBE

HAMWORTHY JUNCTION
Hales Bay Jc.
POOLE
CENTRAL

Goods
HOLTON HEATH
HAMWORTHY
WEST

F
DORCHESTER WEST
DORCHESTER SOUTH
MORETON
WAREHAM
PARKSTONE
BOURNE-MOUTH

Dorchester Jc.
WOOL
Worgret Junc.

Bincombe Tuns.

RADIPOLE
UPWEY & BROADWAY
CORFE CASTLE

TOWN QUAY
SWANAGE

WEYMOUTH

BRISTOL
REDLAND
CLIFTON DOWN
MONTPELIER
STAPLETON RD.

WAPPING WHARF
AVONSIDE WHARF
Gds
Lawrence Hill Jc.

TEMPLE MEADS
Goods
LAWRENCE HILL
Dr Days Bridge Jc.

Ashton Jc.
PYLLE HILL (Gds)
North Somerset Jc.

PARSON STREET
ST. PHILIP'S MARSH

G
BEDMINSTER
Bedminster Jc.

FOUR

5   Ten   4   3   2   1

H I R E

B E R K S H I R E

WARGRAVE
MAIDENHEAD
PANGBOURNE
TILEHURST
West CENTRAL
Jc. East Jc.
TWYFORD
READING
South Jc. GENERAL
READING WEST
THEALE
Southcote
Jc.
EARLEY
WINNERSH
ALDERMASTON
WOKINGHAM
ASCOT
HUNGERFORD
NEWBURY
RACECOURSE
KINTBURY
WELFORD PARK
NEWBURY
THATCHAM
MIDGHAM
BRACKNELL
BEDWYN
MORTIMER
CROWTHORNE
BAGSHOT
SANDHURST
PEWSEY
BRAMLEY
BLACKWATER
CAMBERLEY
FARNBOROUGH
NORTH
FRIMLEY
Pirbright
Jc.
FLEET
FARNBOROUGH
HOOK
WINCHFIELD
Goods
BASINGSTOKE
NORTH CAMP
ASH VALE
LUDGERSHALL
ALDERSHOT
ASH
WHITCHURCH
NORTH
OVERTON
Litchfield Tun.
ANDOVER
Red Posts Jc.
BENTLEY
FARNHAM
GRATELEY
Popham Tuns.
MICHELDEVER
Hindhead
MEDSTEAD &
FOUR MARKS
ALTON
H A M P S H I R E
Waller's Ash Tun.
Winchester Jc. ITCHEN
ABBAS
ROPLEY
ALRESFORD
HASLEMERE
Summit
SALISBURY
(FISHERTON) Fisherton Tun.
Tunnel Jc.
LIPHOOK
WINCHESTER
DEAN
DUNBRIDGE
SHAWFORD
LISS
PETERSFIELD
ROMSEY
Butser Hill
Buriton Tun.
Summit
Allbrook Jc.
Eastleigh S.Jc.
EASTLEIGH
SWAYTHLING
SOUTHAMPTON
AIRPORT
ST.DENYS
REDBRIDGE
TOTTON
BITTERNE
BOTLEY
MILLBROOK
SOUTHAMPTON
CENTRAL
TERMINUS
WOOLSTON
SHOLING
BURSLEDON
S U
LYNDHURST
ROAD
MARCHWOOD
NETLEY
SWAN-
WICK
ROWLAND'S CASTLE
BEAULIEU
ROAD
HAMBLE
HALT
BEDHAMPTON
WARBLINGTON
NUTBOURNE
LAVANT
FAWLEY
FAREHAM
PORTCHESTER
COSHAM
Cosham Jc.
HAVANT
EMSWORTH
BOSHAM
CHICHESTER
FISHBOURNE
SOUTHBOURNE
SOUTHAMPTON
WATER
BEDENHAM
Portcreek Jc.
HILSEA
DRAYTON
BROCKENHURST
Lymington Jc.
PORTSMOUTH
& SOUTHSEA
FRATTON
SWAY
HARBOUR
PORTSMOUTH
HINTON
ADMIRAL
NEW MILTON
LYMINGTON TOWN
LYMINGTON PIER
THE SOLENT
CHRISTCHURCH
POKESDOWN
RYDE
PIER HEAD
ESPLANADE
ST. JOHN'S ROAD
ISLE OF WIGHT
F
BRADING
SANDOWN
SHANKLIN
St. Catherine's Down
G

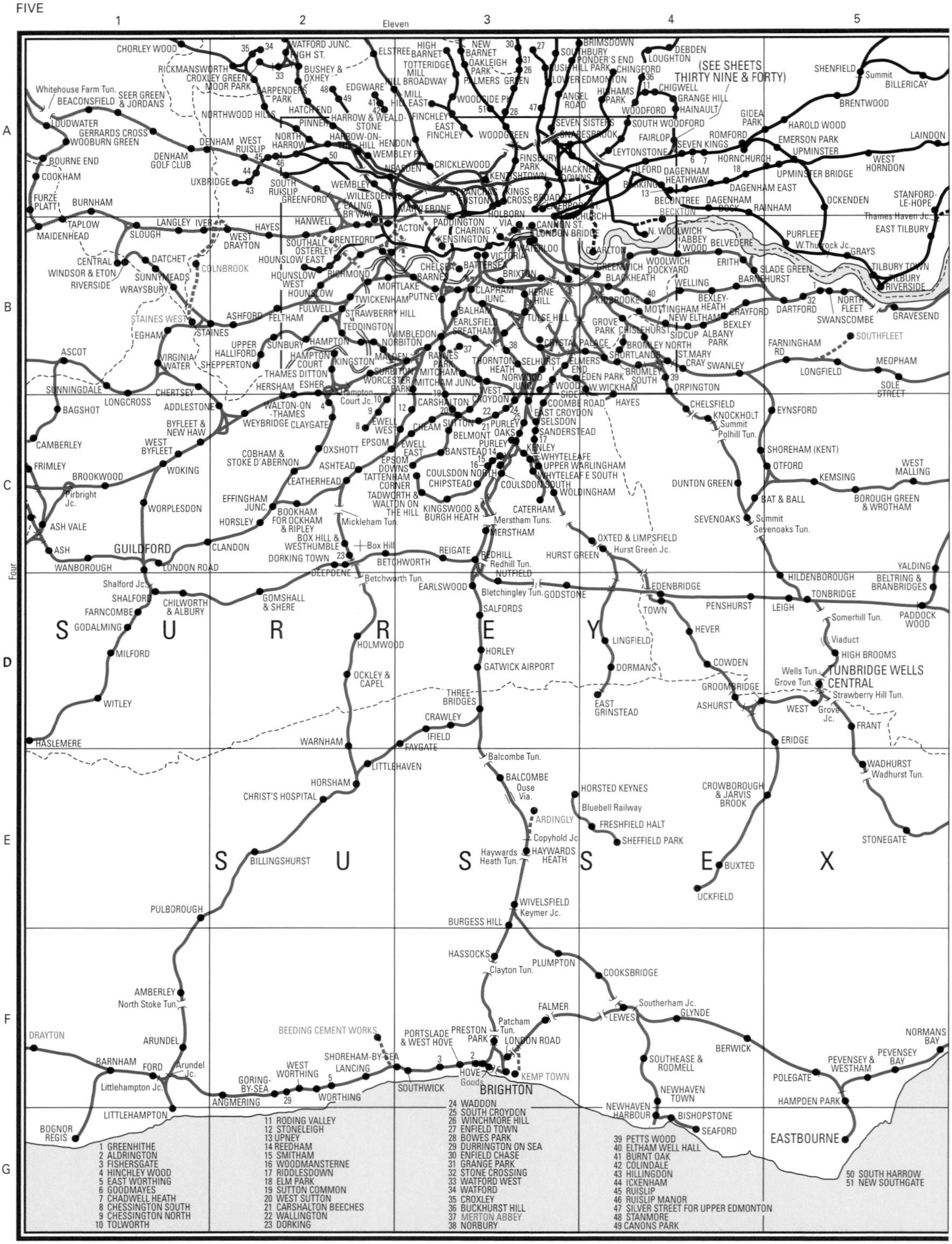
1
2
3
4
5
Eleven
Four
A
B
C
D
E
F
G
SURREY
SUSSEX
(SEE SHEETS THIRTY NINE & FORTY)
CHORLEY WOOD
RICKMANSWORTH
CROXLEY GREEN
MOOR PARK
WATFORD JUNC.
HIGH ST.
BUSHEY & OXHEY
ELSTREE
HIGH BARNET
TOTTERIDGE
MILL HILL BROADWAY
NEW BARNET
OAKLEIGH PARK
PALMERS GREEN
BRIMSDOWN
SOUTHBURY
PONDER'S END
BUSH HILL PARK
LOWER EDMONTON
CHINGFORD
DEBDEN
LOUGHTON
CHIGWELL
GRANGE HILL
HAINAULT
SHENFIELD
Summit
BILLERICAY
BRENTWOOD
GIDEA PARK
HAROLD WOOD
EMERSON PARK
UPMINSTER
LAINDON
ROMFORD
HORNCHURCH
UPMINSTER BRIDGE
WEST HORNDON
OCKENDEN
STANFORD-LE-HOPE
Thames Haven Jc.
EAST TILBURY
PURFLEET
W.Thurrock Jc.
GRAYS
TILBURY TOWN
TILBURY RIVERSIDE
SLADE GREEN
ERITH
BELVEDERE
ABBEY WOOD
N. WOOLWICH
BECKTON
WOOLWICH DOCKYARD
CHARLTON
GREENWICH
BLACKHEATH
KIDBROOKE
WELLING
BEXLEYHEATH
BARNEHURST
DARTFORD
NORTH FLEET
SWANSCOMBE
GRAVESEND
SOUTHFLEET
FARNINGHAM RD
LONGFIELD
MEOPHAM
SOLE STREET
Whitehouse Farm Tun.
BEACONSFIELD
SEER GREEN & JORDANS
LOUDWATER
GERRARDS CROSS
WOOBURN GREEN
BOURNE END
COOKHAM
FURZE PLATT
BURNHAM
TAPLOW
MAIDENHEAD
SLOUGH
LANGLEY
IVER
WEST DRAYTON
HAYES
DENHAM
DENHAM GOLF CLUB
UXBRIDGE
NORTHWOOD HILLS
PINNER
HARROW & WEALDSTONE
WEST RUISLIP
SOUTH RUISLIP
NORTH HARROW
GREENFORD
HANWELL
SOUTHALL
OSTERLEY
BRENTFORD
HOUNSLOW EAST
HOUNSLOW WEST
HOUNSLOW
RICHMOND
WEMBLEY
WILLESDEN JC.
EALING BR'WAY
ACTON
PADDINGTON
MARYLEBONE
EUSTON
ST. PANCRAS
KINGS CROSS
HOLBORN VIA.
CHARING X
CANNON ST.
LONDON BRIDGE
WATERLOO
VICTORIA
KENSINGTON
CHELSEA
BATTERSEA
BRIXTON
CLAPHAM JUNC.
BALHAM
HERNE HILL
TULSE HILL
CRICKLEWOOD
KENTISH TOWN
FINSBURY PARK
WOOD GREEN
FINCHLEY
EAST FINCHLEY
HENDON
SEVEN SISTERS
SNARESBROOK
LEYTONSTONE
ILFORD
BARKING
DAGENHAM HEATHWAY
DAGENHAM EAST
DAGENHAM DOCK
RAINHAM
BECONTREE
SEVEN KINGS
WOODFORD
SOUTH WOODFORD
FAIRLOP
CENTRAL
WINDSOR & ETON RIVERSIDE
DATCHET
SUNNYMEADS
WRAYSBURY
COLNBROOK
STAINES WEST
STAINES
EGHAM
ASHFORD
FELTHAM
SUNBURY
UPPER HALLIFORD
SHEPPERTON
TWICKENHAM
FULWELL
STRAWBERRY HILL
TEDDINGTON
HAMPTON
HAMPTON COURT
THAMES DITTON
KINGSTON
NORBITON
WIMBLEDON
MORTLAKE
BARNES
PUTNEY
EARLSFIELD
STREATHAM
CRYSTAL PALACE
THORNTON HEATH
SELHURST
NORWOOD JUNC.
WEST CROYDON
EAST CROYDON
SOUTH CROYDON
ELMERS END
EDEN PARK
W.WICKHAM
HAYES
BROMLEY SOUTH
BROMLEY NORTH
SHORTLANDS
CHISLEHURST
GROVE PARK
MOTTINGHAM
NEW ELTHAM
SIDCUP
ALBANY PARK
BEXLEY
CRAYFORD
ST.MARY CRAY
SWANLEY
ORPINGTON
CHELSFIELD
KNOCKHOLT
Summit
Polhill Tun.
EYNSFORD
SHOREHAM (KENT)
OTFORD
KEMSING
WEST MALLING
DUNTON GREEN
BAT & BALL
BOROUGH GREEN & WROTHAM
SEVENOAKS
Sevenoaks Tun.
ASCOT
SUNNINGDALE
VIRGINIA WATER
CHERTSEY
ADDLESTONE
LONGCROSS
BAGSHOT
CAMBERLEY
FRIMLEY
BYFLEET & NEW HAW
WEST BYFLEET
WEYBRIDGE
WALTON-ON-THAMES
HERSHAM
ESHER
SURBITON
CLAYGATE
OXSHOTT
COBHAM & STOKE D'ABERNON
EPSOM
EWELL WEST
EWELL EAST
CHEAM
SUTTON
CARSHALTON
MITCHAM
MITCHAM JUNC.
BELMONT
BANSTEAD
PURLEY
PURLEY OAKS
SANDERSTEAD
SELSDON
COOMBE ROAD
KENLEY
WHYTELEAFE
UPPER WARLINGHAM
WHYTELEAFE SOUTH
WOLDINGHAM
COULSDON NORTH
COULSDON SOUTH
CHIPSTEAD
TATTENHAM CORNER
TADWORTH & WALTON ON THE HILL
KINGSWOOD & BURGH HEATH
EPSOM DOWNS
ASHTEAD
LEATHERHEAD
BOOKHAM
FOR OCKHAM & RIPLEY
EFFINGHAM JUNC.
HORSLEY
CLANDON
WOKING
BROOKWOOD
Pirbright Jc.
WORPLESDON
ASH VALE
ASH
WANBOROUGH
GUILDFORD
LONDON ROAD
Mickleham Tun.
BOX HILL & WESTHUMBLE
Box Hill
DORKING TOWN
BETCHWORTH
DEEPDENE
Betchworth Tun.
REIGATE
REDHILL
Redhill Tun.
NUTFIELD
CATERHAM
Merstham Tuns.
MERSTHAM
OXTED & LIMPSFIELD
Hurst Green Jc.
HURST GREEN
EARLSWOOD
Bletchingley Tun.
GODSTONE
EDENBRIDGE
TOWN
PENSHURST
LEIGH
TONBRIDGE
HILDENBOROUGH
YALDING
BELTRING & BRANBRIDGES
PADDOCK WOOD
Somerhill Tun.
Viaduct
HIGH BROOMS
Wells Tun.
Grove Tun.
TUNBRIDGE WELLS CENTRAL
Strawberry Hill Tun.
WEST
Grove Jc.
FRANT
Shalford Jc.
SHALFORD
FARNCOMBE
GODALMING
CHILWORTH & ALBURY
GOMSHALL & SHERE
MILFORD
WITLEY
HASLEMERE
SALFORDS
HORLEY
GATWICK AIRPORT
HOLMWOOD
OCKLEY & CAPEL
LINGFIELD
DORMANS
EAST GRINSTEAD
HEVER
COWDEN
ASHURST
GROOMBRIDGE
ERIDGE
THREE BRIDGES
CRAWLEY
IFIELD
FAYGATE
LITTLEHAVEN
WARNHAM
HORSHAM
CHRIST'S HOSPITAL
Balcombe Tun.
BALCOMBE
Ouse Via.
ARDINGLY
Copyhold Jc.
HORSTED KEYNES
Bluebell Railway
FRESHFIELD HALT
SHEFFIELD PARK
CROWBOROUGH & JARVIS BROOK
WADHURST
Wadhurst Tun.
STONEGATE
BUXTED
UCKFIELD
Haywards Heath Tun.
HAYWARDS HEATH
BILLINGSHURST
PULBOROUGH
WIVELSFIELD
Keymer Jc.
BURGESS HILL
HASSOCKS
Clayton Tun.
PLUMPTON
COOKSBRIDGE
AMBERLEY
North Stoke Tun.
ARUNDEL
Arundel Jc.
DRAYTON
BARNHAM
FORD
Littlehampton Jc.
LITTLEHAMPTON
BOGNOR REGIS
ANGMERING
GORING-BY-SEA
WEST WORTHING
WORTHING
LANCING
SHOREHAM-BY-SEA
BEEDING CEMENT WORKS
SOUTHWICK
PORTSLADE & WEST HOVE
PRESTON PARK
Patcham Tun.
HOVE
Goods
BRIGHTON
LONDON ROAD
KEMP TOWN
FALMER
LEWES
Southerham Jc.
GLYNDE
BERWICK
SOUTHEASE & RODMELL
NEWHAVEN TOWN
NEWHAVEN HARBOUR
BISHOPSTONE
SEAFORD
POLEGATE
PEVENSEY & WESTHAM
PEVENSEY BAY
NORMANS BAY
HAMPDEN PARK
EASTBOURNE
1 GREENHITHE
2 ALDRINGTON
3 FISHERSGATE
4 HINCHLEY WOOD
5 EAST WORTHING
6 GOODMAYES
7 CHADWELL HEATH
8 CHESSINGTON SOUTH
9 CHESSINGTON NORTH
10 TOLWORTH
11 RODING VALLEY
12 STONELEIGH
13 UPNEY
14 REEDHAM
15 SMITHAM
16 WOODMANSTERNE
17 RIDDLESDOWN
18 ELM PARK
19 SUTTON COMMON
20 WEST SUTTON
21 CARSHALTON BEECHES
22 WALLINGTON
23 DORKING
24 WADDON
25 SOUTH CROYDON
26 WINCHMORE HILL
27 ENFIELD TOWN
28 BOWES PARK
29 DURRINGTON ON SEA
30 ENFIELD CHASE
31 GRANGE PARK
32 STONE CROSSING
33 WATFORD WEST
34 WATFORD
35 CROXLEY
36 BUCKHURST HILL
37 MERTON ABBEY
38 NORBURY
39 PETTS WOOD
40 ELTHAM WELL HALL
41 BURNT OAK
42 COLINDALE
43 HILLINGDON
44 ICKENHAM
45 RUISLIP
46 RUISLIP MANOR
47 SILVER STREET FOR UPPER EDMONTON
48 STANMORE
49 CANONS PARK
50 SOUTH HARROW
51 NEW SOUTHGATE

WOODHAM FERRERS
FAMBRIDGE
BATTLESBRIDGE
ALTHORNE
BURNHAM ON CROUCH
WICKFORD
HOCKLEY
RAYLEIGH
ROCHFORD
CHALKWELL
LEIGH ON SEA
BENFLEET FOR CANVEY ISLAND
PRITTLEWELL
PITSEA
THORPE BAY
WESTCLIFF-ON-SEA
SHOEBURYNESS
CORYTON
Canvey Island
SOUTHEND ON SEA VICTORIA
SOUTHEND ON SEA EAST
SOUTHEND ON SEA CENTRAL
THAMESHAVEN

GRAIN
DOCKYARD
SHEERNESS-ON-SEA
Hoo Jc.
HIGHAM
KINGSNORTH
QUEENBOROUGH
Rochester Br. Jc.
STROOD
Fort Pitt Tun.
CHATHAM DOCKYARD
GILLINGHAM
CUXTON
Gillingham Tun.
King's Ferry Bri.
SWALE
ROCHESTER
Chatham Tun.
RAINHAM
KEMSLEY
WESTGATE-ON-SEA
MARGATE
CHATHAM
NEWINGTON
BROADSTAIRS
HALLING
West Jc.   East Jc.
SITTINGBOURNE
TEYNHAM
BIRCHINGTON-ON-SEA
DUMPTON PARK
SNODLAND
CHESTFIELD & SWALECLIFFE
HERNE BAY
Minster East Jc.
Minster West Jc.
RAMSGATE
NEW HYTHE
FAVERSHAM
WHITSTABLE & TANKERTON
MINSTER
EAST MALLING
AYLESFORD
Preston Hall Tuns.
Faversham Jc.
Minster 'B' Jc.
RICHBOROUGH
BARMING
EAST BARRACKS
BEARSTED & THURNHAM
SELLING
STURRY
CANTERBURY
SANDWICH
TOVIL
WEST
MAIDSTONE
HOLLINGBOURNE
Selling Tun.
WEST
EAST
BEKESBOURNE
EAST FARLEIGH
HARRIETSHAM
CHARTHAM
ADISHAM
BETTESHANGER
WATERINGBURY
LENHAM
CHILHAM
AYLESHAM
SNOWDOWN & NONINGTON
DEAL
CHARING
TILMANSTONE COLLIERY
WALMER
MARDEN
HEADCORN
SHEPHERD'S WELL
STAPLEHURST
PLUCKLEY
WYE
MARTIN MILL
ASHFORD
KEARSNEY
Lydden Tun.
Guston Tun.
Buckland Jc.
Charlton Tun.
PRIORY
Harb. Tun.
SANDLING FOR HYTHE
Saltwood Tun.
Archcliffe Jc.
Abbotscliff Tun.
DOVER
Sandling Tun.
CENT.
Martello Tun.
MARINE
WESTENHANGER
WEST
Shakespeare Tun.
TOWN YARD
HARB.
FOLKESTONE
HYTHE
HAM STREET & ORLESTONE
Romney, Hythe & Dymchurch Railway
APPLEDORE
DYMCHURCH
ST MARY'S BAY
NEW ROMNEY
ETCHINGHAM
GREATSTONE
MADDIESON'S CAMP
ROBERTSBRIDGE
RYE
LADE HALT
Mountfield Tun.
WINCHELSEA
DUNGENESS PS
THE PILOT HALT
MOUNTFIELD
DOLEHAM
DUNGENESS
BATTLE
THREE OAKS & GUESTLING
CROWHURST
Bopeep Tunnel
Ore Tun.
WEST ST. LEONARDS
ORE
Mount Pleasant Tun.
Bopeep Jc.
HASTINGS
BEXHILL
Hastings Tun.
ST LEONARDS WARRIOR SQUARE
COLLINGTON HALT
COODEN BEACH

1   2   Thirteen   3   4   Fourteen   5

Cardigan Jc.
WHITLAND
CARMARTHEN

Y Fan Gihirach
SEE SHEET NO.

LLANDEBIE
GWAUN CAE GURWEN
CRAIG-Y-NOS

FERRYSIDE
CWM MAWR
AMMANFORD & TIRYDAIL

A

GREAT MOUNTAIN
AMMANFORD
ABERNANT

ONLLWYN

KIDWELLY
RED BACH
Tycoch Junc.
CYNHEIDRE
PANTYFFYNNON

ABERPERGWM
GLYN NEATH

PEMBREY & BURRY PORT
LLAN-GENNECH
PONTARDULAIS

RESOLVEN

Inset

CLYDACH-ON-TAWE
BLAENANT
GLYNCORRWG
BLAENRHONDDA

CARMARTHEN BAY
LLANELLI
Dock Goods
BYNEA
BRYN-LLIW
LLAN-GYFELACH

BLAENGWYNFI

TREHERBERT

GORSEINON
MORRISTON
NEATH ABBEY
NEATH

CYMMER AFAN
BLAEN GARW

B

GOWERTON
Summit
U.P. BANK
CAERAU
NANTY FFYLLON
CWMDU
PONTY CYMMER
WYNDHAM

SWANSEA HIGH ST.
DAN-Y-GRAIG
BRITON FERRY
MAESTEG
OGMORE

JERSEY MARINE
TROEDYRHIEW GARTH
LLANGYNWYD

PORT TALBOT
DOCK
Margam Junc.
LLANGEINOR

Cefn Junc.

TONDU

Pyle Jt.
Coity Junc.

BRIDGEND

HAVERFORDWEST

NARBERTH

C

JOHNSTON

HERBRANSTON
MILFORD HAVEN
WATERSTON
PEMBROKE DOCK

KILGETTY
SAUNDERSFOOT

PEMBROKE TOWN
LAMPHEY

TENBY

MANORBIER

D

B R I S T O L

ILFRACOMBE

E

Summit
MORTEHOE & WOOLACOMBE

BRAUNTON

WRAFTON
TOWN STA.
BARNSTAPLE

FREMINGTON QUAY
JUNC. STA.
VICTORIA ROAD

F

CHAPELTON

UMBERLEIGH

TORRINGTON
PORTSMOUTH ARMS

KING'S NYMPTON

G

MARLAND

EGGESFORD

PETROCKSTOW

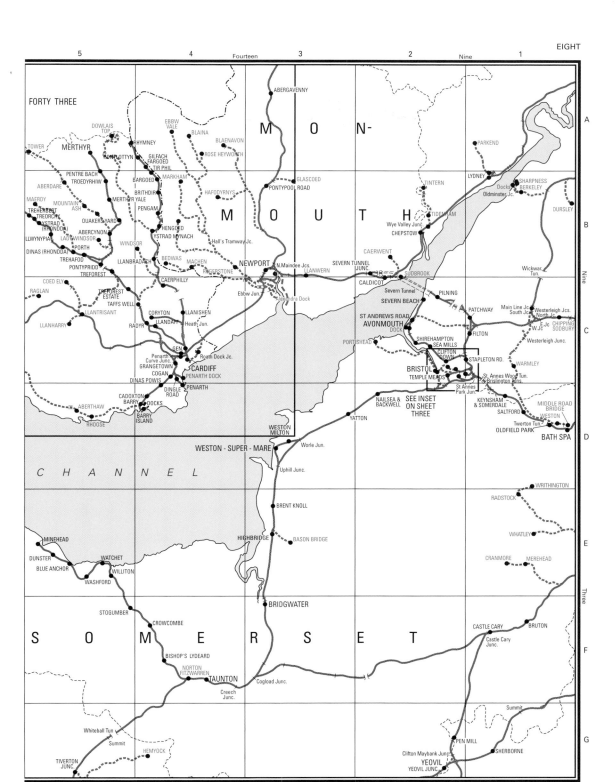

5   4   Fourteen   3   2   Nine   1

FORTY THREE

M O N-

M O U T H

A

B

Nine

C

SEE INSET
ON SHEET
THREE

D

C H A N N E L

WESTON - SUPER - MARE

Writhington

S O M E R S E T

Three

E

F

G

ABERGAVENNY
PARKEND
DOWLAIS TOP
EBBW VALE
BLAINA
RHYMNEY
BLAENAVON
MERTHYR
PONTLOTTYN
ROSE HEYWORTH
TOWER
GILFACH FARGOED
TIR PHIL
MARKHAM
GLASCOED
TINTERN
LYDNEY
SHARPNESS
BERKELEY
Docks
Oldminster Jc.
PENTRE BACH
TROEDYRHIW
BARGOED
PONTYPOOL ROAD
ABERDARE
BRITHDIR
MERTHYR VALE
HAFODYRNYS
DURSLEY
MAERDY
MOUNTAIN ASH
PENGAM
TREHERBERT
TREORCHY
ABERCYNON
QUAKERS YARD
Wye Valley Junc.
TIDENHAM
YSTRAD (RHONDDA)
LADY WINDSOR
HENGOED
CHEPSTOW
LLWYNYPIA
PORTH
WINDSOR
YSTRAD MYNACH
Hall's Tramway Jc.
Wickwar Tun.
DINAS (RHONDDA)
LLANBRADACH
BEDWAS
CAERWENT
TREHAFOD
MACHEN
SEVERN TUNNEL JUNC.
PONTYPRIDD
TREFOREST
NEWPORT
N.Maindee Jcs.
LLANWERN
SUDBROOK
COED ELY
CAERPHILLY
ROGERSTONE
CALDICOT
RAGLAN
TREFOREST ESTATE
Ebbw Jun.
Severn Tunnel
PILNING
LLANTRISANT
TAFFS WELL
Alexandra Dock
SEVERN BEACH
Main Line Jc
South Jc.
Westerleigh Jcs.
North Jc.
CORYTON
LLANISHEN
ST ANDREWS ROAD
PATCHWAY
E.Jc
W.Jc
CHIPPING SODBURY
LLANHARRY
RADYR
LLANDAFF
Heath Jun.
AVONMOUTH DOCK
FILTON
GEN.
SHIREHAMPTON
SEA MILLS
Westerleigh Junc.
PORTISHEAD
CLIFTON DOWN
STAPLETON RD.
WARMLEY
Penarth Curve Junc.
Roath Dock Jc.
GRANGETOWN
CARDIFF
BRISTOL
St. Annes Wood Tun.
COGAN
PENARTH DOCK
TEMPLE MEADS
Brislington Tun.
DINAS POWIS
DINGLE ROAD
St Annes Park Junc.
KEYNSHAM & SOMERDALE
MIDDLE ROAD BRIDGE
CADOXTON
PENARTH
NAILSEA & BACKWELL
SALTFORD
WESTON
ABERTHAW
BARRY DOCKS
Twerton Tun.
RHOOSE
BARRY ISLAND
OLDFIELD PARK
BATH SPA
WESTON MILTON
YATTON
Worle Jun.
Uphill Junc.
RADSTOCK
BRENT KNOLL
WHATLEY
MINEHEAD
HIGHBRIDGE
BASON BRIDGE
CRANMORE
MEREHEAD
DUNSTER
WATCHET
BLUE ANCHOR
WILLITON
WASHFORD
STOGUMBER
BRIDGWATER
CASTLE CARY
BRUTON
CROWCOMBE
Castle Cary Junc.
BISHOP'S LYDEARD
NORTON FITZWARREN
TAUNTON
Cogload Junc.
Creech Junc.
Whiteball Tun.
Summit
Summit
TIVERTON JUNC.
HEMYOCK
PEN MILL
Clifton Maybank Junc.
YEOVIL
YEOVIL JUNC.
SHERBORNE

Two   Three

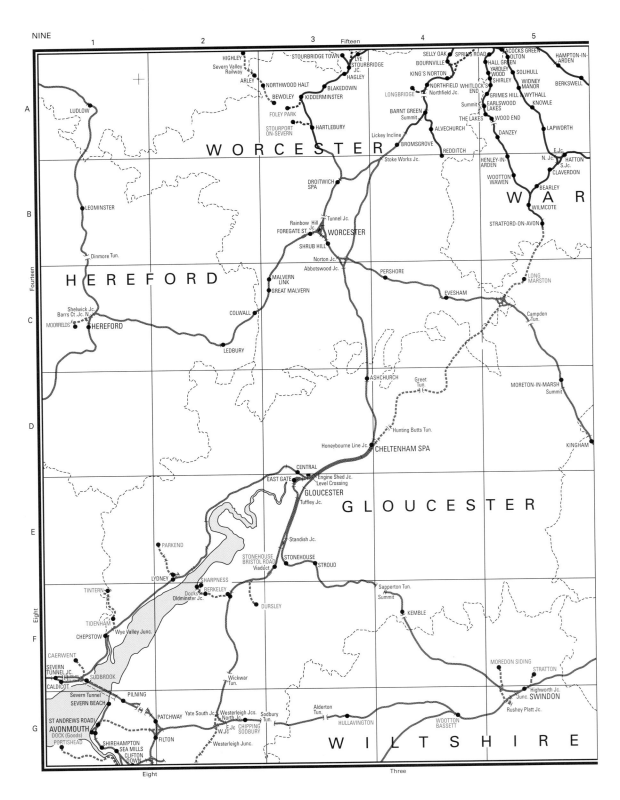

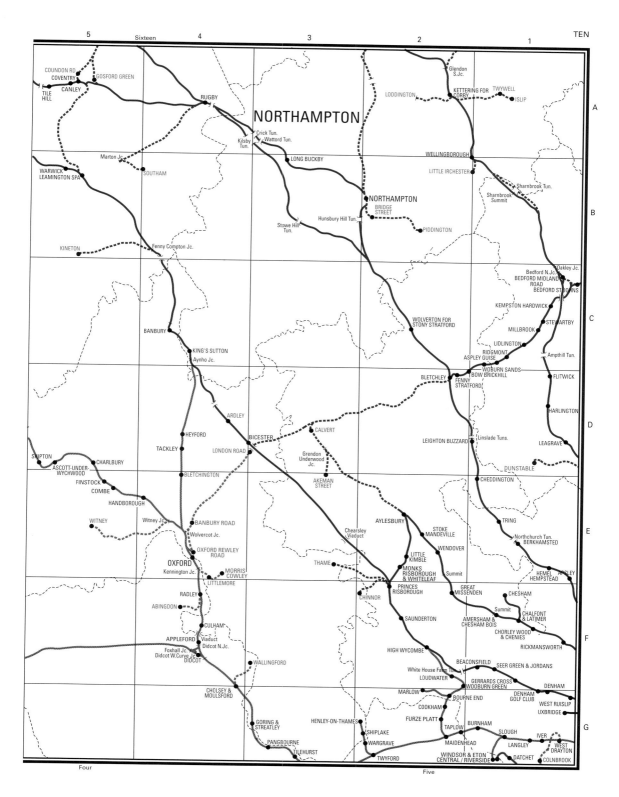

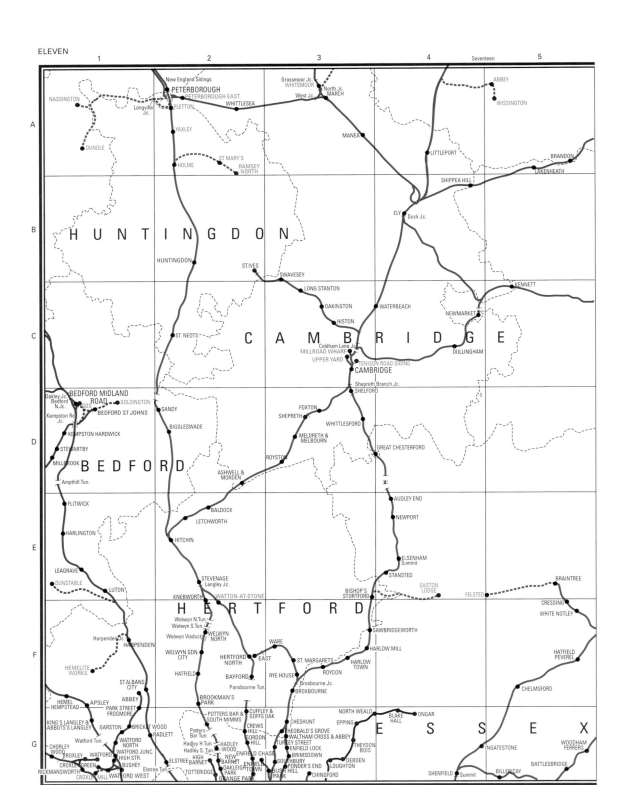

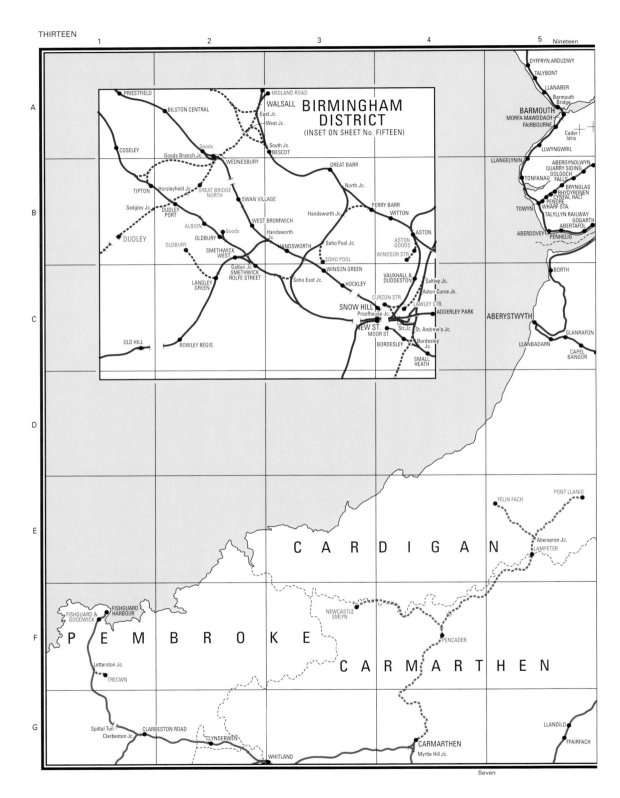

1   2   3   4   5

PRIESTFIELD
BILSTON CENTRAL
COSELEY
MIDLAND ROAD
WALSALL
East Jc.
West Jc.
Goods
Goods Branch Jc.
South Jc.
BESCOT
WEDNESBURY
GREAT BARR

TIPTON
Horsleyfield Jc.
GREAT BRIDGE NORTH
SWAN VILLAGE
North Jc.
Sedgley Jc.
DUDLEY PORT
WEST BROMWICH
Handsworth Jc.
PERRY BARR
WITTON

DUDLEY
ALBION
OLDBURY
Goods
Handsworth Jc.
HANDSWORTH
Soho Pool Jc.
ASTON
ASTON GOODS
OLDBURY
SMETHWICK WEST
WINDSOR STR.

Galton Jc.
SMETHWICK ROLFE STREET
Soho East Jc.
SOHO POOL
WINSON GREEN
VAUXHALL & DUDDESTON
Saltley Jc.
Aston Curve Jc.

LANGLEY GREEN
HOCKLEY
CURZON STR.
SNOW HILL
Proofhouse Jc.
LAWLEY STR.
ADDERLEY PARK
ABERYSTWYTH

OLD HILL
ROWLEY REGIS
NEW ST.
MOOR ST.
Str.Jc. St. Andrew's Jc.
BORDESLEY
Bordesley Jc.
SMALL HEATH

BIRMINGHAM DISTRICT
(INSET ON SHEET No. FIFTEEN)

DYFFRYN ARDUDWY
TALYBONT
LLANABER
Barmouth Bridge
BARMOUTH
MORFA MAWDDACH
FAIRBOURNE
Cader Idris
LLWYNGWRIL

LLANGELYNIN
ABERGYNOLWYN
QUARRY SIDING
DOLGOCH FALLS
TONFANAU
BRYNGLAS
RHYDYRONEN
CYNFAL HALT
PENDRE
WHARF STA.
TOWYN
TALYLLYN RAILWAY
GOGARTH
ABERTAFOL
ABERDOVEY
PENHELIG

BORTH

GLANRAFON
LLANBADARN
CAPEL BANGOR

C A R D I G A N

FELIN FACH
PONT LLANIO

Aberayron Jc.
LAMPETER

FISHGUARD & GOODWICK
FISHGUARD HARBOUR
NEWCASTLE EMLYN

P E M B R O K E

PENCADER

C A R M A R T H E N

Letterston Jc.
TRECWN

LLANDILO

Spittal Tun.
CLARBESTON ROAD
Clarbeston Jc.
CLYNDERWEN
WHITLAND
CARMARTHEN
Myrtle Hill Jc.
FFAIRFACH

A

B

C

D

E

F

G

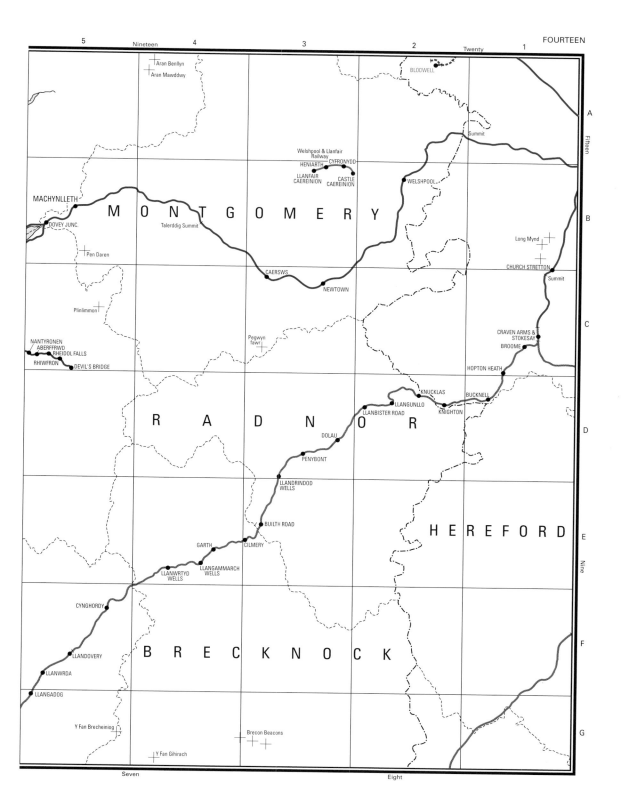

A

Fifteen

B

C

D

E

Nine

F

G

Aran Benllyn
Aran Mawddwy

BLODWELL

Summit

Welshpool & Llanfair
Railway
HENIARTH CYFRONYDD
LLANFAIR CASTLE
CAEREINION CAEREINION
WELSHPOOL

Long Mynd

CHURCH STRETTON
Summit

MACHYNLLETH

M O N T G O M E R Y

DOVEY JUNC.
Talerddig Summit
Pen Daren

CAERSWS
NEWTOWN

CRAVEN ARMS &
STOKESAY
BROOME

Plinlimmon

Pegwyn
fawr

HOPTON HEATH

NANTYRONEN
ABERFFRWD
RHEIDOL FALLS
RHIWFRON
DEVIL'S BRIDGE

KNUCKLAS
LLANGUNLLO BUCKNELL
LLANBISTER ROAD KNIGHTON

R A D N O R

DOLAU

PENYBONT

LLANDRINDOD
WELLS

H E R E F O R D

BUILTH ROAD

GARTH CILMERY

LLANGAMMARCH
WELLS
LLANWRTYD
WELLS

CYNGHORDY

B R E C K N O C K

LLANDOVERY

LLANWRDA

LLANGADOG

Y Fan Brecheiniog

Brecon Beacons

Y Fan Gihirach

1   2   Twenty   3   4   Twenty one   5

A

FARNWORTH & BOLD
HOUGH GN
WIDNES
DITTON
RUNCORN
DOCK
Halton Jc.
Frodsham Jc. Via.
FRODSHAM
INCE & ELTON
HELSBY
FIDLERS FERRY & PENKETH L.L.
WARRINGTON
Old Main Line Jc.
Acton Grange Jc.
ARPLEY
HALE
ALTRINCHAM & BOWDEN
HEALD GREEN
ASHLEY
STYAL
HANDFORTH
MOBBERLEY
KNUTSFORD
WILMSLOW
ADLINGTON
ALDERLEY EDGE
PRESTBURY
Goods
CHEADLE HULME
MIDDLEWOOD
POYNTON
DISLEY
FURNESS VALE
WHALEY BRIDGE
DAVENPORT
HAZEL GROVE
STRINES
NEW MILLS CENTRAL
NEW MILLS NEWTOWN
CHINLEY
Cowburn Tun.
Mam Tor
The Peak
EDALE
HOPE
BAMFORD
HATHERSAGE
(SEE SHEET NO. FORTY FIVE)
Christleton Tun.
Tattenhall Jc.
MOULDS WORTH
DELAMERE
Weaver Jc.
WINNINGTON
ACTON BRIDGE
CUDDINGTON
HARTFORD
LOSTOCK GRALAM
NORTHWICH
HARTFORD & GREENBANK
PLUMLEY
Winsford Jc.
Middlewich
OVER & WHARTON
WINSFORD
GOOSTREY
HOLMES CHAPEL
CHELFORD
MACCLESFIELD
Summit
DOVE HOLES
Chapel-En-Le-Frith Summit
Dove Holes Tun.
PEAK FOREST
Peak Forest
Summit
LADMANLOW (HARPUR HILL)
BUXTON
BUXTON SOUTH
TOPLEY PIKE
TUNSTEAD
HINDLOW
DERBYSHIRE
CHAPEL-EN-LE-FRITH

C H E S H I R E

B

BEESTON CASTLE
SANDBACH
CONGLETON FOR BIDDULPH
LAWTON
ALSAGER
LEEK
Christleton Tun.

Twenty

Chester Line Jc.
Manchester Line Jc.
Shrewsbury Line Jc.
CREWE
N.S. Jc.
RADWAY GREEN
PARK FARM
KIDSGROVE
CHATTERLEY
Cheddleton Jc.
NANTWICH
Curve Jc.
LONGPORT
HOLDITCH
SILVERDALE
ETRURIA
WOLSTANTON
CALDON LOW
WRENBURY
MADELEY
Apedale Jc.
STOKE
OAKAMOOR
CHEADLE

C

Summit
WHITCHURCH
Summit
LONGTON
FLORENCE
BLYTHE BRIDGE
TRENTHAM
WEDGWOOD
BARLASTON & TITTENSOR
HAM HEATH

S T A F F O R D

D

PREES
WEM
STONE
NORTON BRIDGE
UTTOXETER
BURTON-ON-TRENT

S H R O P S H I R E

YORTON
STAFFORD COMMON
STAFFORD
Trent Valley Jc.
Leicester Jc.
Branston Jc.
Birmingham Curve Jc.

E

SHREWSBURY
Curve Jc. E.
ABBEY
ALLSCOTT
The Wrekin
DONNINGTON
GRANVILLE
WELLINGTON
NEW HADLEY
OAKENGATES
HORSEHAY & DAWLEY
Madeley Jc.
WEDNESFIELD
VICTORIA BASIN
WOLVERHAMPTON H.L.
LL Gds.
Gds.
Heath Town Jc.
Crane St. Jc.
MONMORE GN.
PRIESTFIELD
PENKRIDGE
LITTLETON
WEST CANNOCK
LEA HALL
CANNOCK WOOD
Shugborough Tun.
RUGELEY
Wichnor Jc.
T.V. (LOW LEVEL)
LICHFIELD
CITY
FOUR ASHES

Fourteen

F

BAYSTON HILL
Caer Caradoc
IRONBRIDGE
SHIFNAL
COSFORD
ALBRIGHTON
CODSALL
BIRCHES & BILBROOK
Bushbury Jc.
WOLVERHAMPTON
(SEE INSET ON SHEET NO THIRTEEN)
WILLENHALL
BILLSTON STREET
WALSALL
BIRCHILLS
Ryecroft Jc.
Gds.
BESCOT
GREAT BARR
WYLDE GREEN
BLOXWICH
BROWNHILLS
SHENSTONE
TAMWORTH
LL
BLAKE STR.
BUTLERS LANE
FOUR OAKS
SUTTON COLDFIELD
WILNECOTE
KINGSBURY
COLESHILL
CHESTER RD.
WATER ORTON
ERDINGTON

G

CHURCH STRETTON
BRIDGNORTH
EARDINGTON
HAMPTON LOADE
Severn Valley Railway
HIGHLEY
SHUT END
ROUND OAK
BRIERLEY HILL
CRADLEY HEATH
STOURBRIDGE TOWN
STOURBRIDGE JC.
DUDLEY
TIPTON
COSELEY
SWAN VILL
WEST BROM.
SPON LANE
OLDBURY
LANGLEY GREEN
ROWLEY REGIS
OLD HILL
LYE
KINGS HEATH
SELLY OAK
SOHO
WINSON GREEN
NEW STREET
MOOR STREET
MOOR ST.
WITTON
ASTON
HOCKLEY
SNOW
ADDERLEY PARK
SMALL HEATH
SPRINGFIELD
BOLTON
HALL GREEN
BIRMINGHAM
STECHFORD
LEA HALL
MARSTON GREEN
TYSELEY
ACOCKS GREEN
HAMPTON-IN-ARDEN
GRAVELLY HILL
CASTLE BROMWICH
PERRY BARR
WYLDE GREEN

Nine

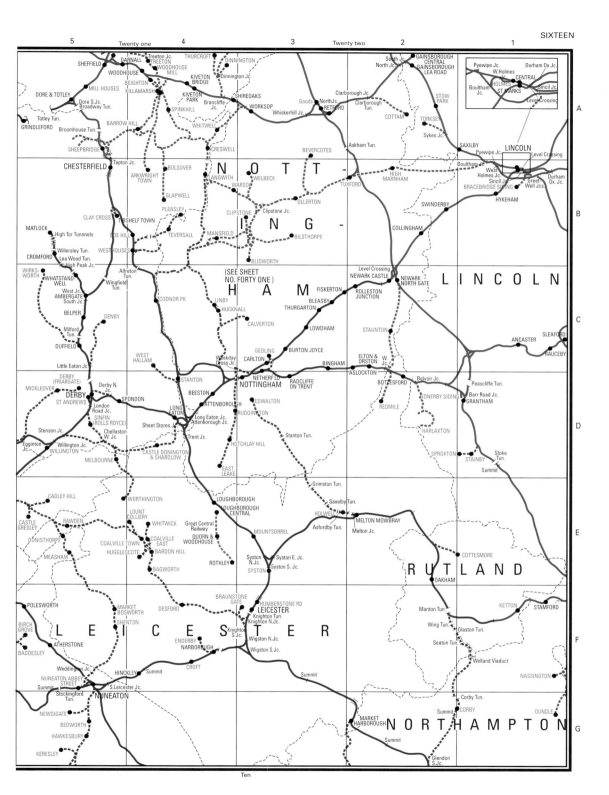

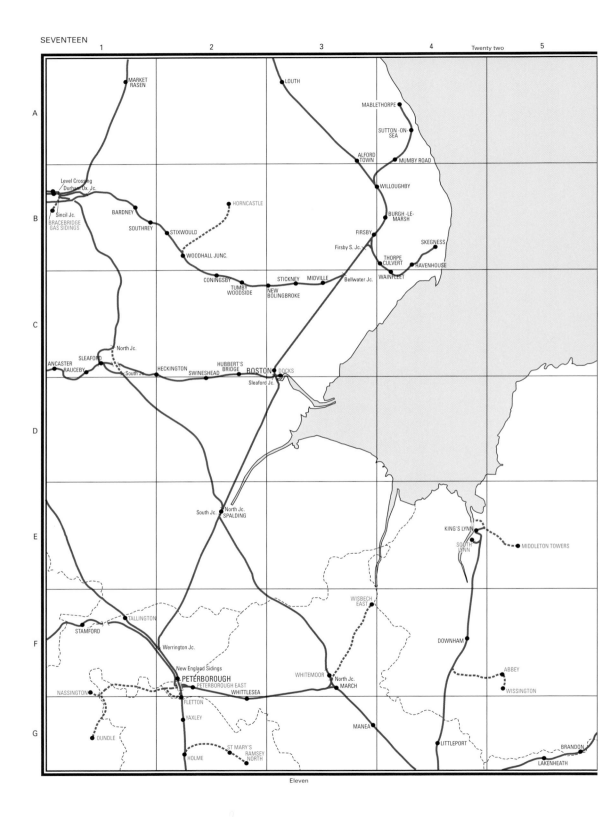

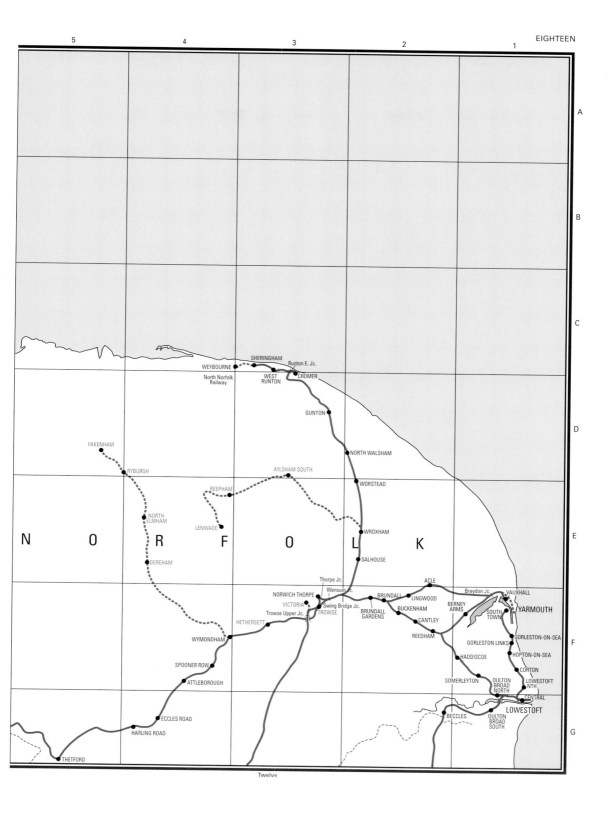

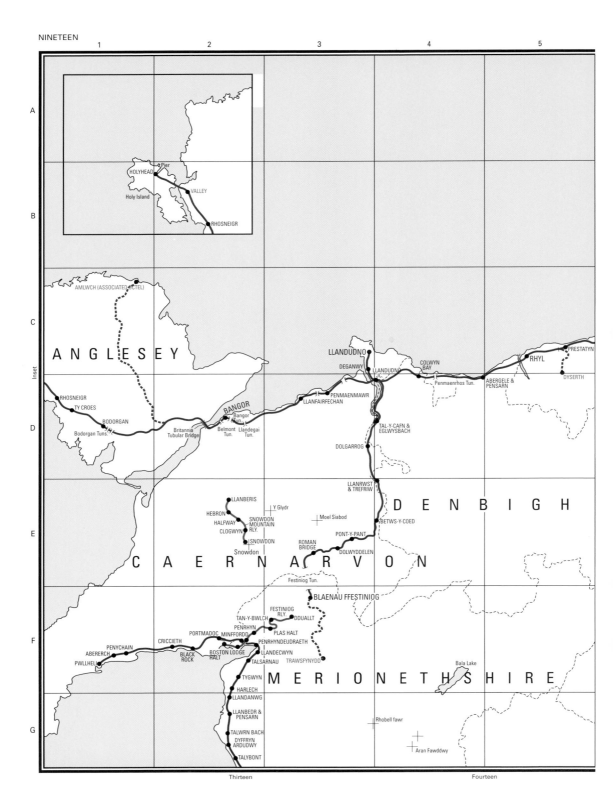

1   2   3   4   5

A

HOLYHEAD
Pier
VALLEY
Holy Island
RHOSNEIGR

B

AMLWCH (ASSOCIATED OCTEL)

C

A N G L E S E Y

LLANDUDNO
DEGANWY
LLANDUDNO JC.
COLWYN BAY
Penmaenrhos Tun.
RHYL
PRESTATYN
ABERGELE & PENSARN
DYSERTH

RHOSNEIGR
TY CROES
BODORGAN
Bodorgan Tuns.
BANGOR
Bangor Tun.
Britannia Tubular Bridge
Belmont Tun.
Llandegai Tun.
PENMAENMAWR
LLANFAIRFECHAN
TAL-Y-CAFN & EGLWYSBACH
DOLGARROG

D

LLANRWST & TREFRIW

LLANBERIS
HEBRON
HALFWAY
CLOGWYN
SNOWDON MOUNTAIN RLY.
SNOWDON
Snowdon
Y Glydr
Moel Siabod
BETWS-Y-COED
PONT-Y-PANT
ROMAN BRIDGE
DOLWYDDELEN

D E N B I G H

E

C A E R N A R V O N

Festiniog Tun.
BLAENAU FFESTINIOG

F

TAN-Y-BWLCH
FESTINIOG RLY.
DDUALLT
PENRHYN
PLAS HALT
PORTMADOC MINFFORDD
CRICCIETH
PENYCHAIN
ABERERCH
PWLLHELI
BLACK ROCK
BOSTON LODGE HALT
PENRHYNDEUDRAETH
LLANDECWYN
TALSARNAU
TRAWSFYNYDD

Bala Lake

M E R I O N E T H S H I R E

TYGWYN
HARLECH
LLANDANWG
LLANBEDR & PENSARN
TALWRN BACH
DYFFRYN ARDUDWY
TALBONT

Rhobell fawr

Aran Fawddwy

G

Thirteen   Fourteen

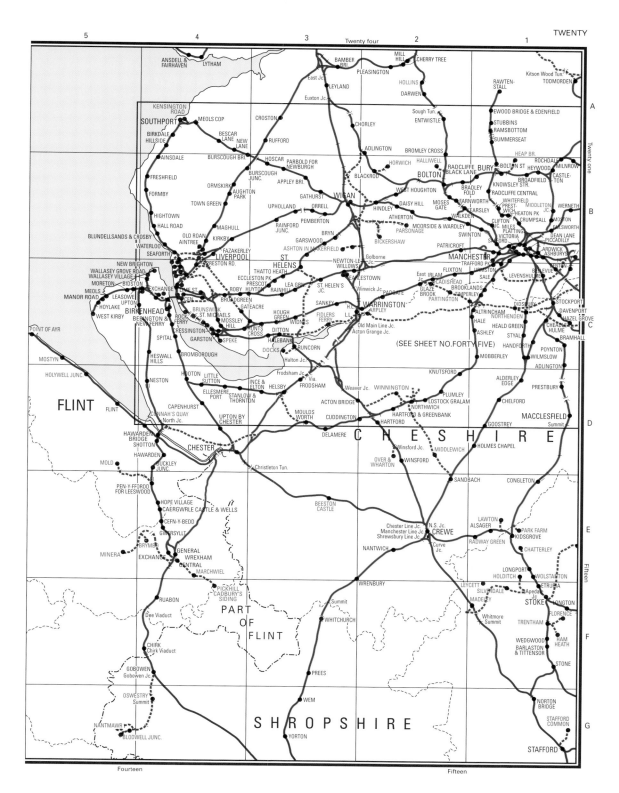

5   4   3   Twenty four   2   1

Twenty one

ANSDELL & FAIRHAVEN
LYTHAM
MILL HILL
BAMBER BRI.
CHERRY TREE
PLEASINGTON
East Jc.
LEYLAND
Euxton Jc.
HOLLINS
DARWEN
KENSINGTON ROAD
CROSTON
CHORLEY
SOUGH TUN.
ENTWISTLE
RAWTEN-STALL
TODMORDEN
Kitson Wood Tun.

SOUTHPORT
MEOLS COP
RUFFORD
ADLINGTON
BROMLEY CROSS
EWOOD BRIDGE & EDENFIELD
STUBBINS
RAMSBOTTOM
SUMMERSEAT

BIRKDALE
HILLSIDE
BESCAR LANE
NEW LANE
HORWICH
HALLIWELL
HEAP BR.
RADCLIFFE
BLACK LANE
BOLTON ST.
HEYWOOD
ROCHDALE
MILNROW

AINSDALE
BURSCOUGH BRI.
HOSCAR
PARBOLD FOR NEWBURGH
BLACKROD
WEST HOUGHTON
BOLTON
BRADLEY FOLD
KNOWSLEY STR.
BROADFIELD
CASTLE-TON

FRESHFIELD
BURSCOUGH JUNC.
APPLEY BRI.
WIGAN
FARNWORTH
RADCLIFFE CENTRAL

FORMBY
ORMSKIRK
AUGHTON PARK
GATHURST
ORRELL
HINDLEY
DAISY HILL
ATHERTON
MOSES GATE
WHITEFIELD
PREST-WICH
MIDDLETON JC.
WERNETH

TOWN GREEN
UPHOLLAND
PEMBERTON
MOORSIDE & WARDLEY
PARSONAGE
WALKDEN
FEARLEY
CRUMPSALL
MORTON
FAILSWORTH

HIGHTOWN
HALL ROAD
MAGHULL
RAINFORD JUNC.
BRYN
BICKERSHAW
SWINTON
CLIFTON JC.
MILES PLATTING
VICTORIA
DEAN LANE
PICCADILLY

BLUNDELLSANDS & CROSBY
OLD ROAN
AINTREE
KIRKBY
GARSWOOD
PATRICROFT
MANCHESTER
ARDWICK
ASHBURYS

WATERLOO
SEAFORTH
FAZAKERLEY
LIVERPOOL
ASHTON IN MAKERFIELD
Golborne
TRAFFORD PK.
LEVENSHULME
BELLE VUE

NEW BRIGHTON
PRESTON RD.
ST. HELENS
NEWTON-LE-WILLOWS
FLIXTON
East IRLAM Jc.
CLADISHEAD
SALE
STOCKPORT

WALLASEY GROVE ROAD
WALLASEY VILLAGE
EXCHANGE
LIME ST.
THATTO HEATH
EARLESTOWN
GLAZE BROOK
BROOKLANDS
TIMPERLEY
DAVENPORT

MORETON
BIDSTON
OPEN
ECCLESTON PK.
PRESCOT
ST. HELEN'S JC.
WINWICK Jc.
PADGATE
PARTINGTON
HAZEL GROVE

MEOLS
LEASOWE
UPTON
ROBY
HUYTON
RAINHILL
LEA GRN.
WARRINGTON
ALTRINCHAM
NORTHENDEN
DIDSBURY
CHEADLE HULME

MANOR ROAD
BIRKENHEAD
BROADGREEN
SANKEY
APPLEY
HEALD GREEN
BRAMHALL

HOYLAKE
WEST KIRBY
BEBINGTON & NEW FERRY
ROCK FERRY
BRUNSWICK
ST. MICHAELS
GATEACRE
HOUGH GREEN
FIDLERS FERRY
H.L. LL.
HALE
ASHLEY
STYAL
HANDFORTH

SPITAL
CRESSINGTON
MOSSLEY HILL
WIDNES
Old Main Line Jc.
Acton Grange Jc.
MOBBERLEY
POYNTON
WILMSLOW

POINT OF AYR
HESWALL HILLS
GARSTON
SPEKE
DITTON
HALEBANK
DOCKS
RUNCORN
(SEE SHEET NO. FORTY FIVE)
ADLINGTON

MOSTYN
BROMBOROUGH
Halton Jc.
KNUTSFORD
ALDERLEY EDGE
PRESTBURY

HOLYWELL JUNC.
NESTON
HOOTON
LITTLE SUTTON
Frodsham Jc.
Via. FRODSHAM
WEAVER Jc.
WINNINGTON
WINNINGTON
PLUMLEY
CHELFORD

FLINT
FLINT
ELLESMERE PORT
STANLOW & THORNTON
HELSBY
ACTON BRIDGE
LOSTOCK GRALAM
NORTHWICH
MACCLESFIELD

CAPENHURST
MOULDS WORTH
CUDDINGTON
HARTFORD & GREENBANK
HARTFORD
GOOSTREY
Summit

CANNAH'S QUAY
North Jc.
UPTON BY CHESTER
DELAMERE
C H E S H I R E

HAWARDEN BRIDGE
SHOTTON
CHESTER
MIDDLEWICH
HOLMES CHAPEL

MOLD
HAWARDEN
Winsford Jc.
OVER & WHARTON
WINSFORD

BUCKLEY JUNC.
Christleton Tun.
SANDBACH
CONGLETON

PEN-Y-FFORDD FOR LEESWOOD
HOPE VILLAGE
CAERGWRLE CASTLE & WELLS
BEESTON CASTLE
LAWTON
ALSAGER
PARK FARM
KIDSGROVE

CEFN-Y-BEDD
GWERSYLLT
Chester Line Jc.
Manchester Line Jc.
Shrewsbury Line Jc.
CREWE
RADWAY GREEN
CHATTERLEY

BRYMBO
GENERAL
WREXHAM
CENTRAL
NANTWICH
Curve Jc.
LONGPORT
HOLDITCH
WOLSTANTON

MINERA
EXCHANGE
MARCHWIEL
LEYCETT
SILVERDALE
MADELEY
Apedale Jc.
ETRURIA
STOKE

PICKHILL
CADBURY'S SIDING
WRENBURY
LONGTON
FLORENCE

RUABON
Summit
WHITMORE Summit
TRENTHAM
HAM HEATH

PART OF FLINT
Dee Viaduct
WHITCHURCH
PREES
WEDGWOOD
BARLASTON & TITTENSOR
STONE

CHIRK
Chirk Viaduct
WEM
NORTON BRIDGE

GOBOWEN
Gobowen Jc.
YORTON
STAFFORD COMMON

OSWESTRY
Summit
S H R O P S H I R E
STAFFORD

NANTMAWR
BLODWELL JUNC.

Fourteen   Fifteen

1   2   3   Twenty eight   4   5

A   B   Twenty four   Inset   C   D   Twenty   E   F   G

REDMIRE   LEYBURN   NORTHALLERTON South Jc.

STALYBRIDGE
ASHTON UNDER LYNE
GUIDE BRIDGE
Denton Jc.

THIRSK

YORK
Poppleton Jc.
Severus Jc.
Goods
North Jc.
Ho Igate Bridge Jc.
Burton Lane Jc.
Foss Islands Jc.
LAYERTHORPE
FOSS ISLAND (Goods)
Chaloners Whin Jc.

LEEDS
WELLINGTON
CITY
Wortley Jc.
ARMLEY Wortley W. Jct.
Canal Jc. Leeds Jc.
HUNSLET LANE
COPLEY HILL
Wortley S. Jc.
Engine Shed Jc.

RYLSTONE
GARGRAVE
KNARESBOROUGH
Goods
STARBECK
HAMMERTON
CATTAL
HARROGATE

Skipton N. Jc.
SKIPTON
PANNAL
WEETON

YORK
Bootham Jc.
Burton Lane Jc.
POPPLETON
Poppleton Jc.
Severus Jc.
Holgate Bridge Jc.
Chaloners Whin Jc.
LAYERTHORPE
MURTON LANE
OSBALDWICK
DUNNINGTON
ELVINGTON
Derwent Valley Light Railway

BEN RHYDDING
BURLEY-IN-WHARFEDALE
ILKLEY
MENSTON
GUISELEY
Bramhope Tun. Summit

Worth Valley Bch Jc.
KEIGHLEY
HORSFORTH
ULLESKELF

INGROW
DAMEMS
OAKWORTH
BINGLEY
Bingley Tun.
Keighley & Worth Valley Railway
HAWORTH
OXENHOPE

SHIPLEY
FRIZINGHALL
HEADINGLEY
MARSH LANE
CHURCH FENTON
E. Jc.
Swing Bri.
SELBY
Brayton N. Jc.

FORSTER SQUARE
EXCHANGE
BRADFORD
NEW PUDSEY
WORTLEY
LEEDS
Gds. Hunslet Bch Jc.
HUNSLET
Stourton Jc.
CROSSGATES
GARFORTH
MICKLEFIELD
SOUTH MILFORD
Milford Jc.
Gascoigne Wood Jc.

DUDLEY HILL
WOODLES-FORD
LEDSTON LUCK
BARLOW
WRESSLE

Wyke Tun.
MORLEY LOW
BOWERS ROW
DRAX

Weasal Hall Tun.
HEBDEN BRI.
Hall Royd Jc.
Millwood Tun.
Horsfall Tun.
Castle Hill Tun.
MYTHOLMROYD
N. BRIDGE
LIVERSEDGE
NEWMARKET COLLIERY
ALTOFTS
METHLEY
CASTLEFORD
MONKHILL
FERRYBRIDGE
KNOTTINGLEY
WHITLEY BRIDGE
HENSALL
SNAITH
RAWCLIFFE

TODMORDEN
HALIFAX
Bank House Tun.
BRIGHOUSE
BATLEY
NORMANTON
PONTEFRACT
BAGHILL

Winterbutlee Tun.
SOWERBY BRI.
GREETLAND
ELLAND
Bradley Wood Tun.
DEWSBURY
WAKE-FIELD
Summit Tun.
MIRFIELD
L.N.W. Jc.
HORBURY
SHARLSTON
ACKWORTH
ASKERN
THORNE NORTH
THORNE SOUTH

LITTLEBOROUGH
DEIGHTON
Springwood Jc.
LOCKWOOD
HUDDERSFIELD
Crigglestone Tun.

ROCHDALE
Rochdale E. Jc.
MILNROW
MARSDEN
Standedge Tun.
HONLEY
BROCKHOLES
Robin Hood Tun.
STOCKSMOOR
SHEPLEY
CLAYTON WEST
DARTON
MOORTHORPE
SOUTH ELMSALL
Askern Jc.
Shaftholme Jc.
Joan Croft Jc.
Adwick Jc.
Skellow Jc.
BULLCROFT
Kirk Sandall Jc.
Bentley Jc.
Thorne Jc.
STAINFORTH & HATFIELD

NEW HEY
SHAW & CROMPTON
Thurstonland Tun.
SKELMANTHORPE
MONK BRETTON
HICKLETON
GRIMETHORPE
FRICKLEY
BRODSWORTH

ROYTON JUNC.
DENBY DALE
Cumberworth Tun.
BARNSLEY
DODWORTH
DARFIELD
BARNBURGH
DONCASTER

OLDHAM
MUMPS
WERNERTH
HOLLINWOOD
GREENFIELD
Scout Tunnel
Wellhouse Tun.
Barnsley Jc.
WOMBWELL
BOLTON ON DEARNE
MEXBOROUGH
Low Ellers Jc.
Bessacar Jc.

ASHTON
MOSSLEY
STALEY & MILLBROOK
Woodhead Tun.
PENISTONE
Thurgoland Tun.
ROCKINGHAM
ELSECAR
Wath Rd. Jc.
St. Catherine's Jcs.
Low Ellers Jc.
SWINTON
CONISBORO.
ROSSINGTON
Loversall Carr Jc.

STALYBRIDGE
GUIDE BRIDGE
HYDE NORTH
NEWTON
Dinting Via.
ARKSEY
Kirk Sandall Jc.
York Rd.
Bentley Jc.
WHEATLEY PARK
DEEPCAR
Tankersley Tun.
CHAPELTOWN
KILNHURST
MALTBY

DENTON
Denton Jc.
DUKINFIELD
HADFIELD
DINTING
GLOSSOP CENTRAL
DONCASTER
North Jc.
MARSH GATE (Gds)
CHAPELTOWN
ECCLESFIELD
ROTHERHAM
ROTHERHAM CENTRAL
SILVERWOOD
HARWORTH

HYDE CENTRAL
Reddish
Apethorne Jc.
WOODLEY
BROAD-BOTTOM
Balby
South Jc.
OUGHTY BRIDGE
WADSLEY BRIDGE

BREDBURY
ROMILEY
Hexthorpe Jc.
S. Jc.
Potteric Carr Jc.
Low Ellers Jc.
Bessaoar Jc.
THURCROFT
HARWORTH

STOCK-PORT
ROSE HILL
MARPLE
Hexthorpe
Doncaster Avoiding Line Jc.
Black Carr Jc.
Lowersall Carr Jc.
ATTERCLIFFE
DARNALL
TINSLEY
TREETON
Treeton Jc.
WOODHOUSE MILL
Dinnington Jc.

DAVEN-PORT
HAZEL GROVE
STRINES
YORKS MAIN
Black Carr E. Jc.
St. Catherine's Jcs.
SHEFFIELD
MIDLAND
WOODHOUSE
Southern Jc.

SEE SHEET NO.FORTY TWO

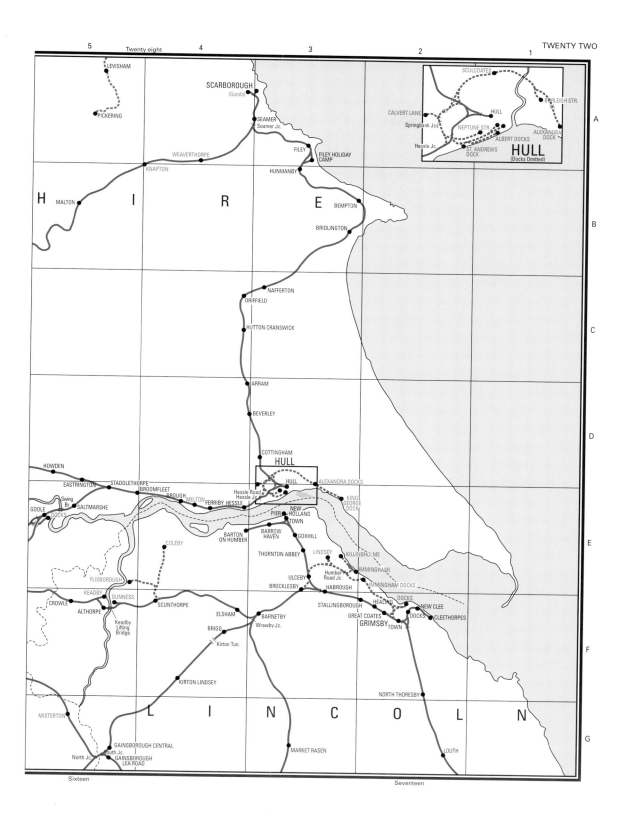

5   Twenty eight   4   3   2   1

LEVISHAM

SCARBOROUGH
(Goods)

PICKERING

SEAMER
Seamer Jc.

WEAVERTHORPE

FILEY
FILEY HOLIDAY
CAMP

KNAPTON

HUNMANBY

H   I   R   E

MALTON

BEMPTON

BRIDLINGTON

NAFFERTON

DRIFFIELD

HUTTON CRANSWICK

ARRAM

BEVERLEY

COTTINGHAM

HULL

HOWDEN

EASTRINGTON   STADDLETHORPE
BROOMFLEET
GOOLE   BROUGH   MELTON   HULL   Alexandra Docks
Swing   SALTMARSHE   FERRIBY HESSLE   Hessle Road   KING
Br.   DOCKS   Hessle Jc.   GEORGE
NEW   DOCK
PIER   HOLLAND
TOWN

BARTON   BARROW
ON HUMBER   HAVEN   GOXHILL

COLEBY   THORNTON ABBEY   LINDSEY   KILLINGHOLME

HUMBER   (IMMINGHAM)
Road Jc.

FLIXBOROUGH   ULCEBY   IMMINGHAM DOCKS

KEADBY   BROCKLESBY   HABROUGH

CROWLE   GUNNESS   SCUNTHORPE   STALLINGBOROUGH   HEALING   DOCKS   NEW CLEE
ALTHORPE   DOCKS   CLEETHORPES
Keadby   ELSHAM   GREAT COATES
Lifting   BARNETBY   GRIMSBY TOWN
Bridge   Wrawby Jc.

BRIGG
Kirton Tun.

KIRTON LINDSEY

MISTERTON   L   I   N   C   O   L   N

NORTH THORESBY

GAINSBOROUGH CENTRAL
North Jc.   South Jc.
GAINSBOROUGH   MARKET RASEN   LOUTH
LEA ROAD

Sixteen   Seventeen

HULL inset (Docks Omitted)

SCULCOATES

BURLEIGH STR.

CALVERT LANE   HULL
Springbank Jcs   NEPTUNE STR   ALEXANDRA
Hessle Jc.   ALBERT DOCKS   DOCK
ST. ANDREWS
DOCK   HULL
(Docks Omitted)

A

B

C

D

E

F

G

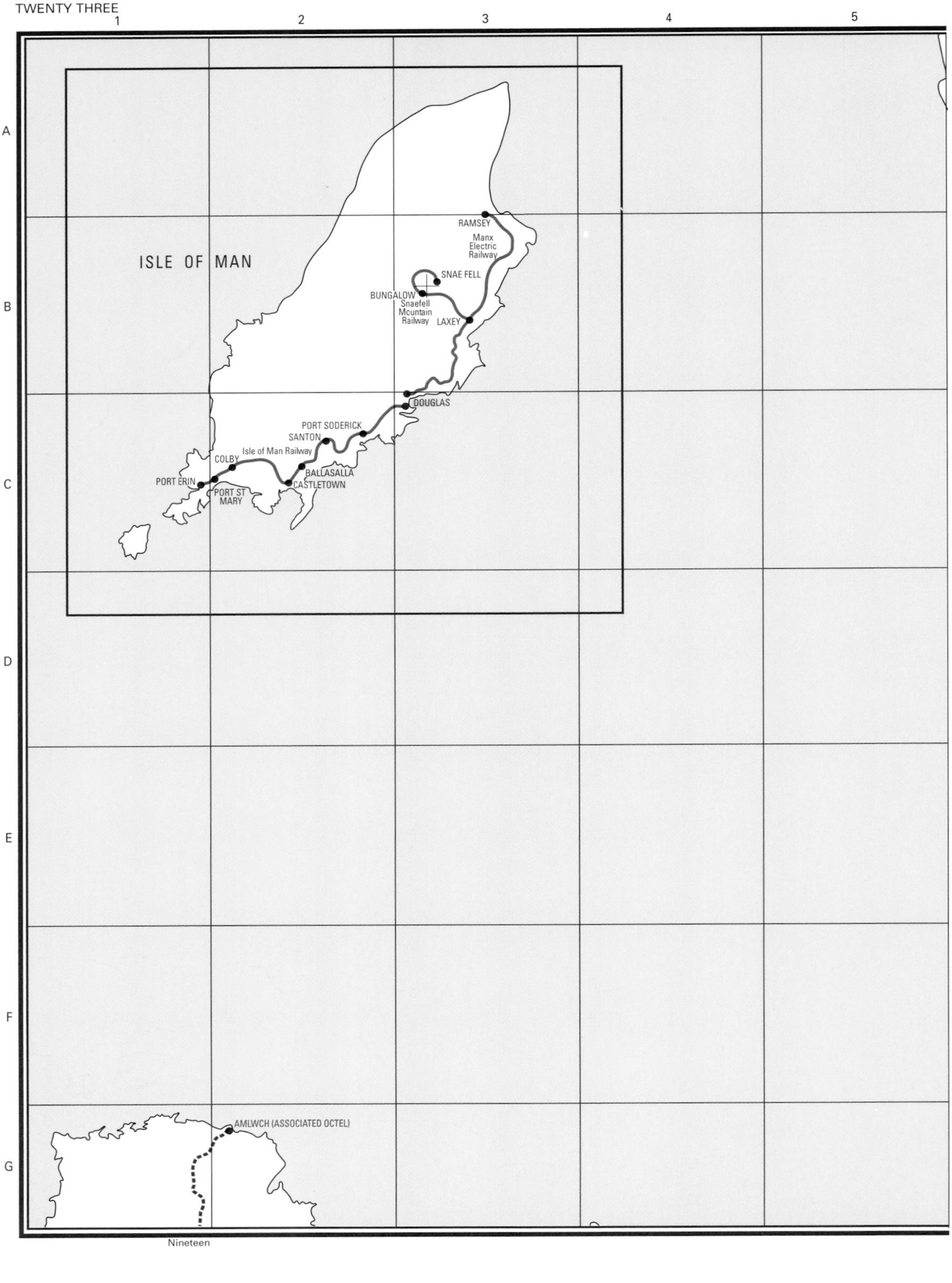

1   2   3   4   5

A

ISLE OF MAN

RAMSEY
Manx
Electric
Railway
SNAE FELL
BUNGALOW
Snaefell
Mountain
Railway
LAXEY

B

DOUGLAS

PORT SODERICK
SANTON
COLBY   Isle of Man Railway
PORT ERIN   BALLASALLA
PORT ST   CASTLETOWN
MARY

C

D

E

F

AMLWCH (ASSOCIATED OCTEL)

G

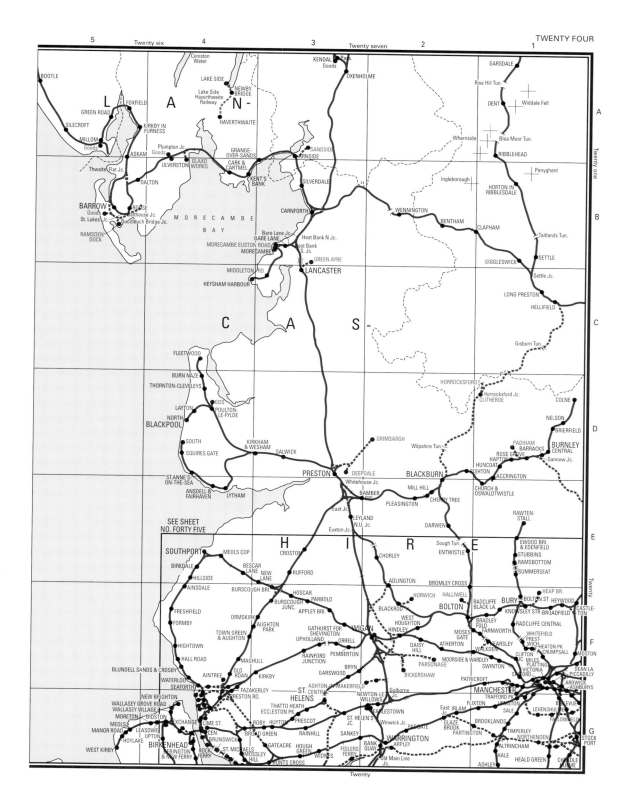

5   Twenty six   4   3   Twenty seven   2   1

BOOTLE

Coniston Water

KENDAL Pass.
Goods

GARSDALE

OXENHOLME

Rise Hill Tun.

LAKE SIDE

NEWBY BRIDGE

FOXFIELD

Lake Side
Haverthwaite
Railway

DENT

Widdale Fell

L A N-

GREEN ROAD

HAVERTHWAITE

SILECROFT

KIRKBY IN FURNESS

Whernside

Blea Moor Tun.

MILLOM
Goods

Plumpton Jc.
Goods

GRANGE-OVER-SANDS

SANDSIDE

ARNSIDE

RIBBLEHEAD

ASKAM

GLAXO WORKS

CARK & CARTMEL

ULVERSTON

Ingleborough

Penyghent

Thwaite Flat Jc.

DALTON

KENT'S BANK

SILVERDALE

HORTON IN RIBBLESDALE

BARROW
Goods

ROOSE

Saltmouse Jc.

St. Lukes Jc.

Buccleuch Bridge Jc.

M O R E C A M B E

B A Y

CARNFORTH

WENNINGTON

BENTHAM

CLAPHAM

Taitlands Tun.

RAMSDEN DOCK

Bare Lane Jc.

BARE LANE

Hest Bank N Jc.

GIGGLESWICK

SETTLE

MORECAMBE EUSTON ROAD

Hest Bank

MORECAMBE

S. Jc.

GREEN AYRE

MIDDLETON RD

Settle Jc.

HEYSHAM HARBOUR

LANCASTER

LONG PRESTON

HELLIFIELD

C A S-

Gisburn Tun.

FLEETWOOD

HORROCKSFORD

BURN NAZE

Horrocksford Jc.

COLNE

THORNTON-CLEVELEYS

CLITHEROE

LAYTON

GDS

NELSON

POULTON-LE-FYLDE

BRIERFIELD

NORTH
BLACKPOOL

PADIHAM

BARRACKS

BURNLEY CENTRAL

SOUTH

KIRKHAM & WESHAM

SALWICK

GRIMSARGH

Wilpshire Tun.

ROSE GROVE

HAPTON

Gannow Jc.

SQUIRES GATE

HUNCOAT

RISHTON

ACCRINGTON

ST.ANNE'S-ON-THE-SEA

PRESTON

DEEPDALE

BLACKBURN

Whitehouse Jc.

MILL HILL

CHURCH & OSWALDTWISTLE

ANSDELL & FAIRHAVEN

LYTHAM

BAMBER BRI

CHERRY TREE

PLEASINGTON

East Jc.

RAWTEN-STALL

SEE SHEET
NO. FORTY FIVE

LEYLAND
N.U. Jc.

DARWEN

Euxton Jc.

H   I   R   E

SOUTHPORT

MEOLS COP

CROSTON

CHORLEY

Sough Tun.

ENTWISTLE

EWOOD BRI. & EDENFIELD

BIRKDALE

BESCAR LANE

RUFFORD

STUBBINS

NEW LANE

RAMSBOTTOM

HILLSIDE

SUMMERSEAT

AINSDALE

BURSCOUGH BRI.

ADLINGTON

BROMLEY CROSS

HEAP BR.

HOSCAR

HORWICH

HALLIWELL

BURY

FRESHFIELD

BURSCOUGH JUNC.

PARBOLD

BLACKROD

RADCLIFFE
BLACK LA.

BOLTON ST

HEYWOOD

CASTLE-TON

APPLEY BRI.

WEST HOUGHTON

KNOWSLEY STR.

BROADFIELD

FORMBY

ORMSKIRK

BOLTON

ORMSKIRK

GATHURST FOR SHEVINGTON

WIGAN

BRADLEY FOLD

FARNWORTH

RADCLIFFE CENTRAL

TOWN GREEN & AUGHTON

AUGHTON PARK

UPHOLLAND

ORRELL

HINDLEY

MOSES GATE

WHITEFIELD

PREST-WICH

HEATON PK

MOSTON

HIGHTOWN

RAINFORD JUNCTION

PEMBERTON

DAISY HILL

ATHERTON

MOORSIDE & WARDLEY

WALKDEN

CLIFTON

CRUMPSALL

HALL ROAD

MAGHULL

BRYN

SWINTON

JC. MILES PLATTING

VICTORIA

DEAN LA.

PICCADILLY

BLUNDELL SANDS & CROSBY

OLD ROAN

GARSWOOD

PARSONAGE

SALFORD

ARDWICK

ASHBURYS

WATERLOO

AINTREE

KIRKBY

BICKERSHAW

PATRICROFT

SEAFORTH

FAZAKERLEY

ST. CENTRAL

ASHTON-IN-MAKERFIELD

MANCHESTER

TRAFFORD PK

NEW BRIGHTON

PRESTON RD.

ST.
HELENS

NEWTON-LE-WILLOWS

Golborne Jc.

FLIXTON

URMSTON

SALE

LEVENSHULME

BELLE VUE

WALLASEY GROVE ROAD

WALLASEY VILLAGE

THATTO HEATH

EARLESTOWN

East Jc.

IRLAM Jc.

MORETON

BIDSTON

ECCLESTON PK

Winwick Jc.

PADGATE

BROOKLANDS

FALLOWFIELD

MEOLS

EXCHANGE

LIME ST.

ROBY

HUYTON

PRESCOT

ST. HELEN'S
JC.

SANKEY

GLAZE BROOK

PARTINGTON

TIMPERLEY

NORTHENDEN

STOCK-PORT

MANOR ROAD

LEASOWE

UPTON

CEN

BRUNSWICK

BROAD GREEN

RAINHILL

BANK QUAY

WARRINGTON

ALTRINCHAM

HEALD GREEN

CHEADLE HULME

HOYLAKE

BIRKENHEAD

ROCK FERRY

ST. MICHAELS

GATEACRE

HOUGH GREEN

FIDLERS FERRY

ARPLEY

HALE

WEST KIRBY

BEBINGTON & NEW FERRY

MOSSLEY HILL

WIDNES

Old Main Line

ASHLEY

HUNTS CROSS

Twenty

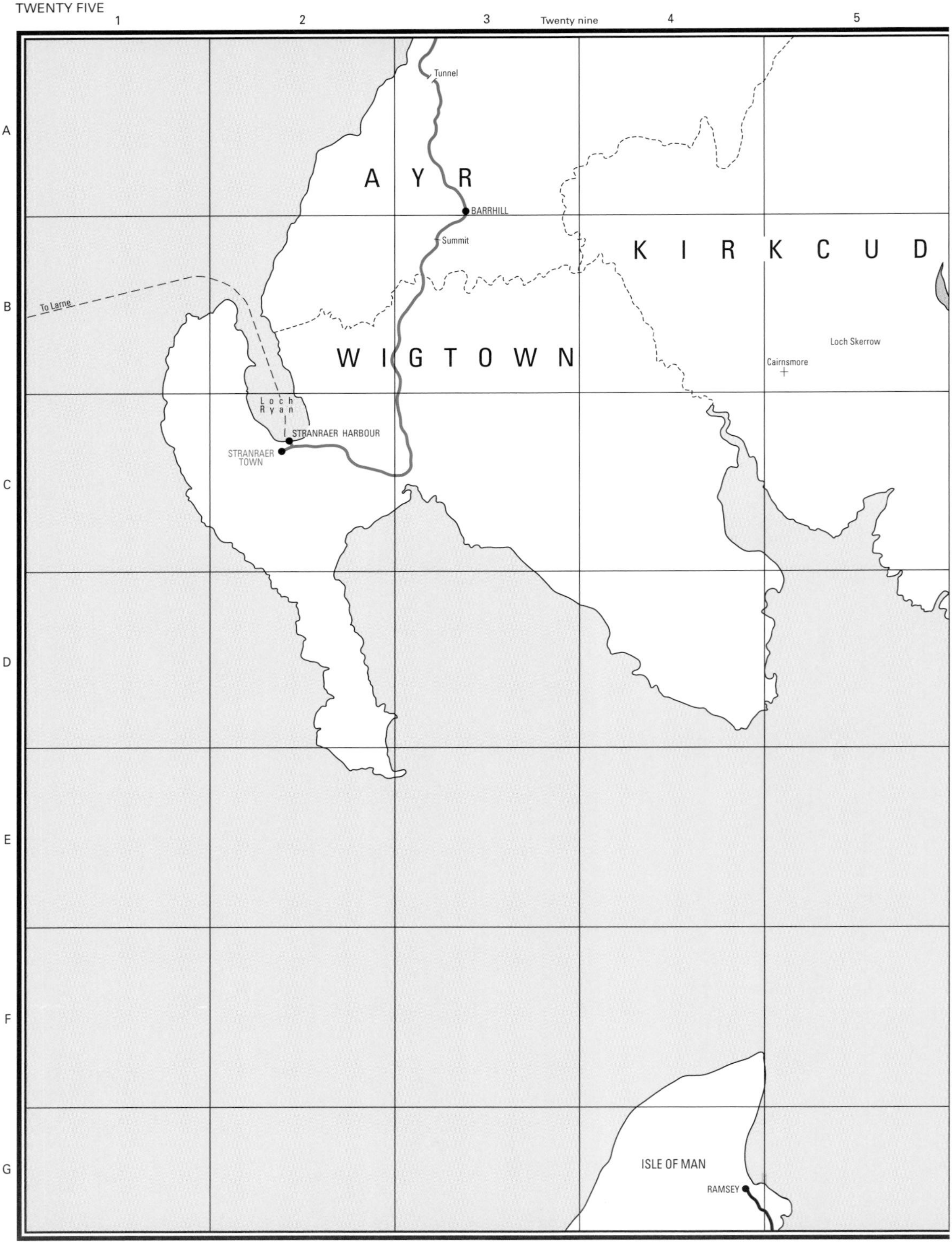

1   2   3   4   5

A

Tunnel

A Y R

BARRHILL

Summit

K I R K C U D

B

To Larne

Loch Skerrow

W I G T O W N

Cairnsmore

Loch
Ryan

STRANRAER HARBOUR

STRANRAER
TOWN

C

D

E

F

G

ISLE OF MAN

RAMSEY

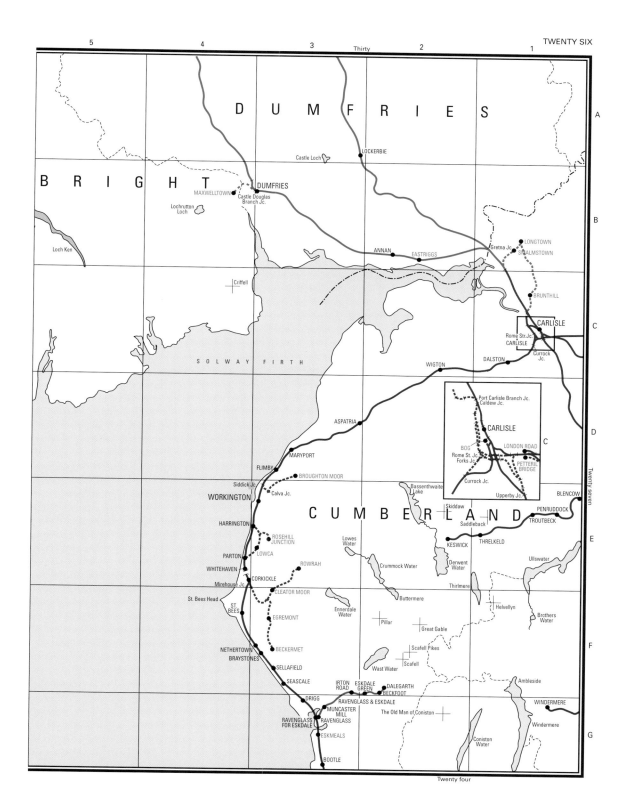

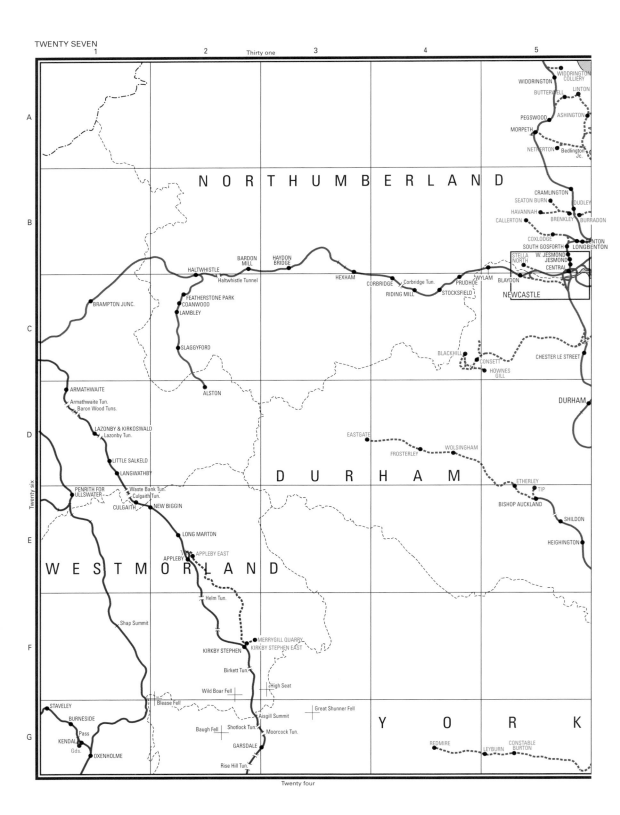

NORTHUMBERLAND

WIDDRINGTON COLLIERY
WIDDRINGTON
BUTTERWELL LINTON
PEGSWOOD ASHINGTON
MORPETH
NETHERTON Bedlington Jc.

CRAMLINGTON
SEATON BURN DUDLEY
HAVANNAH
CALLERTON BRENKLEY BURRADON
COXLODGE BENTON
SOUTH GOSFORTH LONGBENTON
STELLA NORTH W. JESMOND JESMOND
CENTRAL

BARDON MILL HAYDON BRIDGE
HALTWHISTLE
Haltwhistle Tunnel HEXHAM
CORBRIDGE Corbridge Tun. PRUDHOE WYLAM
RIDING MILL STOCKSFIELD BLAYDON
NEWCASTLE

FEATHERSTONE PARK
BRAMPTON JUNC. COANWOOD
LAMBLEY

BLACKHILL
CONSETT CHESTER LE STREET
HOWNES GILL

SLAGGYFORD

C

ARMATHWAITE
Armathwaite Tun. ALSTON
Baron Wood Tuns.

DURHAM

LAZONBY & KIRKOSWALD
Lazonby Tun.

EASTGATE

LITTLE SALKELD WOLSINGHAM
LANGWATHBY FROSTERLEY

D

PENRITH FOR ETHERLEY
ULLSWATER Waste Bank Tun. TIP
CULGAITH Culgaith Tun. BISHOP AUCKLAND
NEW BIGGIN SHILDON

LONG MARTON HEIGHINGTON

E

WESTMORLAND APPLEBY EAST
APPLEBY

Helm Tun.

Shap Summit

MERRYGILL QUARRY
KIRKBY STEPHEN KIRKBY STEPHEN EAST

F

Birkett Tun.

Wild Boar Fell High Seat

STAVELEY Great Shunner Fell
BURNESIDE Bleale Fell YORK
Pass Aisgill Summit
KENDAL Baugh Fell Shotlock Tun. REDMIRE CONSTABLE BURTON
Gds. Moorcock Tun. LEYBURN
OXENHOLME GARSDALE

G

Rise Hill Tun.

Twenty six

Twenty four

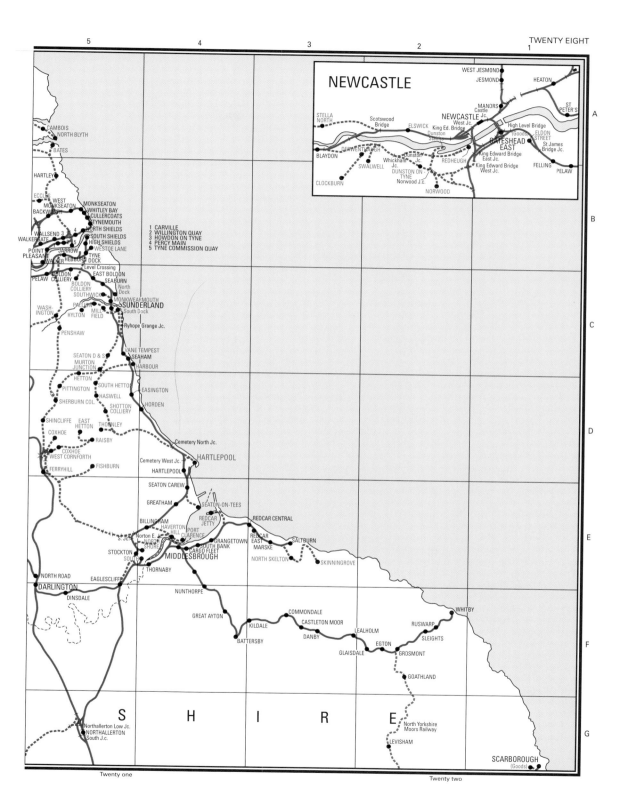

5   4   3   2   1

NEWCASTLE

WEST JESMOND
JESMOND
HEATON
MANORS
Castle
NEWCASTLE
West Jc.
ST
PETER'S
STELLA
NORTH
Scotswood
Bridge
ELSWICK
King Ed. Bridge
Dunston
(Goods)
High Level Bridge
ELDON
STREET
GATESHEAD
EAST
St James
Bridge Jc.
DERWENTHAUGH
Dunston
King Edward Bridge
East Jc.
BLAYDON
Whickham
Jc.
Dunston
Jc.
REDHEUGH
King Edward Bridge
West Jc.
FELLING
SWALWELL
DUNSTON ON
TYNE
PELAW
CLOCKBURN
Norwood J.c.
NORWOOD

A

CAMBOIS
NORTH BLYTH
BATES

B

HARTLEY

1 CARVILLE
2 WILLINGTON QUAY
3 HOWDON ON TYNE
4 PERCY MAIN
5 TYNE COMMISSION QUAY

ECCLES
WEST
MONKSEATON
BACKWORTH
MONKSEATON
WHITLEY BAY
CULLERCOATS
TYNEMOUTH
NORTH SHIELDS
WALLSEND 3   4
WALKERGATE   5
SOUTH SHIELDS
HIGH SHIELDS
WESTOE LANE
POINT
PLEASANT
JARROW
TYNE
DOCK
WALKER HEBBURN
Level Crossing
PELAW COLLIERY
EAST BOLDON
BOLDON
SEABURN
BOLDON
COLLIERY
North
Dock
SOUTHWICK
MONKWEARMOUTH
WASH-
INGTON
PALLION
SUNDERLAND
South Dock
HYLTON
MILL
FIELD
Ryhope Grange Jc.

C

PENSHAW
VANE TEMPEST
SEATON D & S
MURTON
JUNCTION
SEAHAM
HARBOUR
HETTON
SOUTH HETTON
EASINGTON
PITTINGTON
HASWELL
SHERBURN COL.
SHOTTON
COLLIERY
HORDEN
SHINCLIFFE
EAST
HETTON
THORNLEY
COXHOE
RAISBY

D

Cemetery North Jc.
COXHOE
WEST CORNFORTH
FISHBURN
Cemetery West Jc.
HARTLEPOOL
FERRYHILL
HARTLEPOOL
SEATON CAREW

GREATHAM
SEATON-ON-TEES
REDCAR CENTRAL
BILLINGHAM
HAVERTON
HILL
REDCAR
JETTY
PORT
CLARENCE
GRANGETOWN
REDCAR
EAST
SALTBURN

E

St JC.
Norton E. J.
NORTH
SHORE
SOUTH BANK
MARSKE
STOCKTON
SOUTH
CARGO FLEET
NORTH SKELTON
SKINNINGROVE
THORNABY
MIDDLESBROUGH
NORTH ROAD
EAGLESCLIFFE
DARLINGTON
DINSDALE
NUNTHORPE
WHITBY
GREAT AYTON
COMMONDALE
RUSWARP
KILDALE
CASTLETON MOOR
LEALHOLM
BATTERSBY
DANBY
EGTON
SLEIGHTS
GLAISDALE
GROSMONT

F

GOATHLAND

S   H   I   R   E
North Yorkshire
Moors Railway
Northallerton Low Jc.
NORTHALLERTON
South J.c.
LEVISHAM

G

SCARBOROUGH
(Goods)

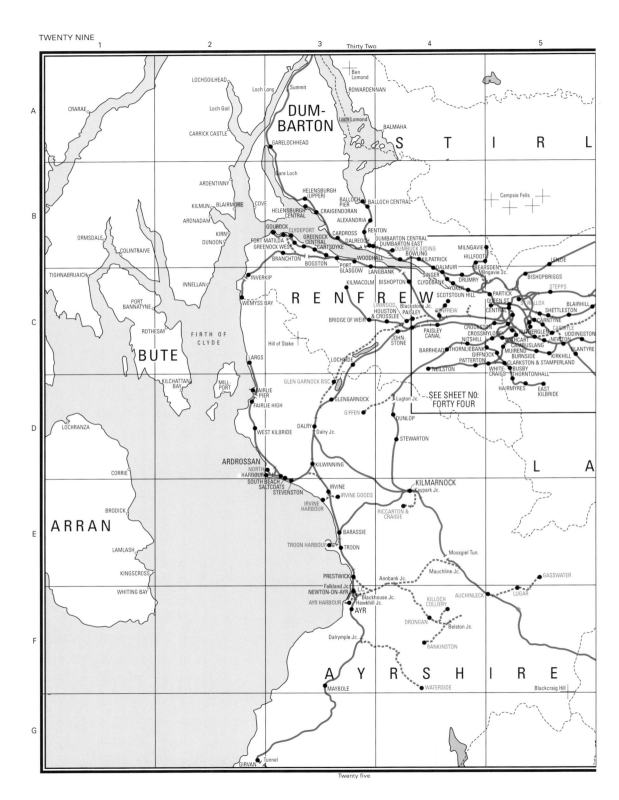

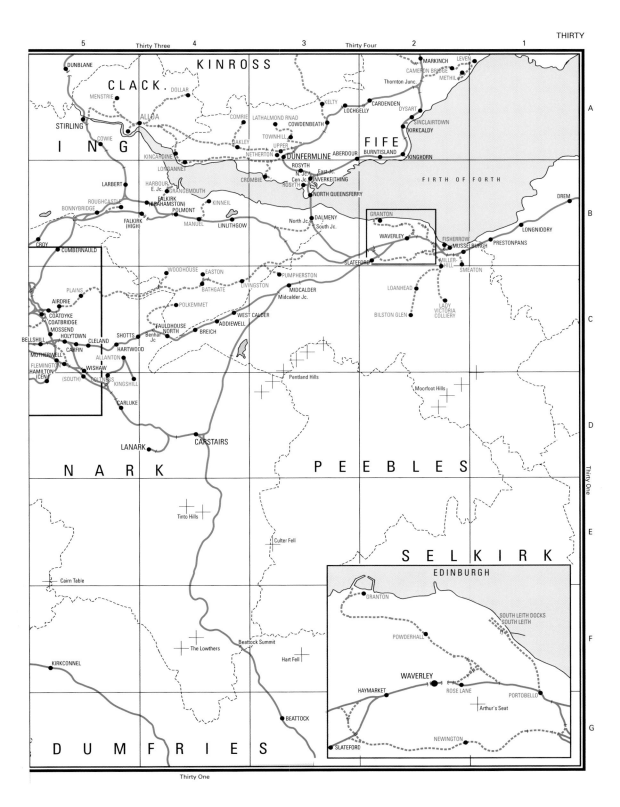

DUNBLANE

KINROSS

CLACK.

DOLLAR

MENSTRIE

ALLOA

STIRLING

COWIE

ING

N

G

KINCARDINE

LONGANNET

LARBERT

HARBOUR
E. Jc.

ROUGHCASTLE

BONNYBRIDGE

FALKIRK
(GRAHAMSTON)

POLMONT

FALKIRK
(HIGH)

KINNEIL

MANUEL

LINLITHGOW

CROY

CUMBERNAULD

PLAINS

AIRDRIE

COATDYKE
COATBRIDGE
MOSSEND

BELLSHILL   HOLYTOWN
CLELAND

MOTHERWELL   CARFIN

FLEMINGTON   ALLANTON
HAMILTON   WISHAW
(CEN.)

(SOUTH)   COLTNESS

KINGSHILL

CARLUKE

LANARK

N   A   R   K

KELTY

COMRIE   LATHALMOND RNAD

TOWNHILL

OAKLEY   UPPER
NETHERTON

COWDENBEATH

LOCHGELLY

CARDENDEN

FIFE

ABERDOUR   BURNTISLAND

DUNFERMLINE

ROSYTH
N. Jc.   East Jc.
Cen Jc.   INVERKEITHING
CROMBIE   ROSYTH

NORTH QUEENSFERRY

North Jc.   DALMENY
South Jc.

LINLITHGOW

WOODHOUSE   EASTON

BATHGATE

POLKEMMET

FAULDHOUSE
NORTH

ADDIEWELL   BREICH

Benhar
Jc.

SHOTTS

HARTWOOD

LIVINGSTON

PUMPHERSTON

MIDCALDER
Midcalder Jc.

WEST CALDER

CARSTAIRS

P   E   E   B   L   E   S

Pentland Hills

Tinto Hills

Culter Fell

Cairn Table

MARKINCH   LEVEN

CAMERON BRIDGE   METHIL

Thornton Junc.

DYSART

SINCLAIRTOWN

KIRKCALDY

KINGHORN

FIRTH OF FORTH

DREM

GRANTON

WAVERLEY

SLATEFORD

FISHERROW
MUSSELBURGH   LONGNIDDRY

PRESTONPANS

MILLER
HILL   SMEATON

LOANHEAD

BILSTON GLEN

LADY
VICTORIA
COLLIERY

Moorfoot Hills

S   E   L   K   I   R   K

EDINBURGH

GRANTON

SOUTH LEITH DOCKS
SOUTH LEITH

POWDERHALL

WAVERLEY

HAYMARKET

ROSE LANE

PORTOBELLO

Arthur's Seat

SLATEFORD

NEWINGTON

The Lowthers   Beattock Summit

Hart Fell

KIRKCONNEL

BEATTOCK

D   U   M   F   R   I   E   S

A

B

C

D

E

F

G

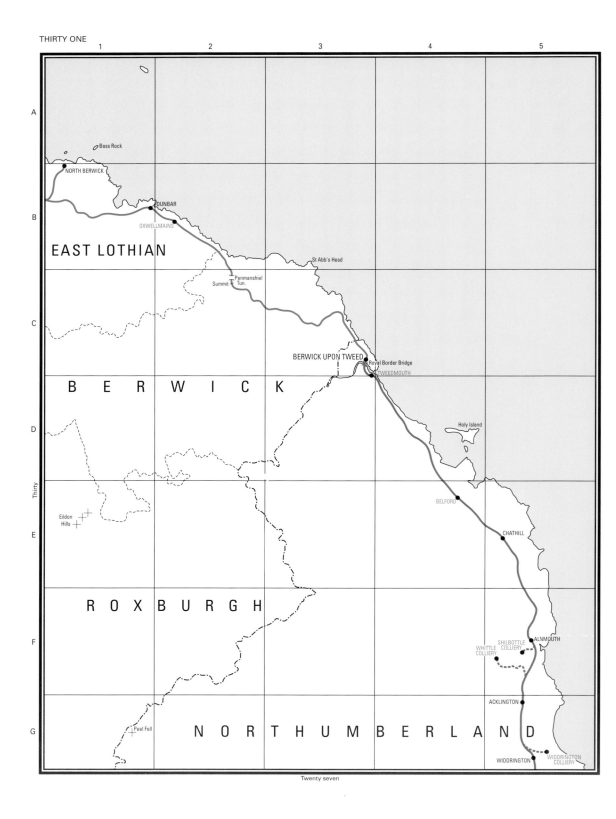

1   2   3   4   5

A

Bass Rock
NORTH BERWICK

DUNBAR
B   OXWELLMAINS

EAST LOTHIAN

St Abb's Head

Penmanshiel
Summit   Tun.

C

BERWICK UPON TWEED
Royal Border Bridge
TWEEDMOUTH

B E R W I C K

Holy Island

D

Thirty

BELFORD

Eildon
Hills

CHATHILL
E

R O X B U R G H

SHILBOTTLE
COLLIERY   ALNMOUTH
WHITTLE
COLLIERY
F

Peel Fell   N O R T H U M B E R L A N D

ACKLINGTON

G

WIDDRINGTON
COLLIERY
WIDDRINGTON

5   4   3   Thirty five   2   1

A

I N V E R N E S S

Loch Garry
Loch Oich
Corrieyairock Hill

MALLAIG
MORAR
Loch Morar
Loch Lochy
Loch Arkaig

B

ARISAIG
BEASDALE
LOCHAILORT
GLENFINNAN
Loch nan Uamh
Loch Ailort
LOCHEILSIDE   ANNAT   CORPACH
SPEAN BRIDGE   TULLOCH
ROY BRIDGE
Beinn Odhar
Loch Eil
BANAVIE
LOCHABER
Mallaig Jc.
FORT WILLIAM
Aonach Mor
Carn Dearg
Loch Treig
Summit
Loch Ossian

C

Loch Shiel
Ben Nevis
CORROUR
Leim Uilleim
Acharacle Pier
Ben Resipol
Bidean nam Bian
RANNOCH
Creach Bheinn
Creag Ghorm
Buchaille Etive
Loch Laidon

D

Loch Linnhe
Beinn Donn
Stob Ghabbar
Gorton Crossing
Rannoch Moor
Loch Tulla
BRIDGE OF ORCHY
Bienn Dòrain

E

Loch Creran
Beinn Bhreac
Loch Etive
Summit
Beinn Challum
CONNEL FERRY
Ben Cruachan
Glenlochy Crossing
Summit
TYNDRUM UPPER
TYNDRUM LOWER
OBAN
Glencruitten Summit
TAYNUILT
Pass of Brander
DALMALLY
Beinn Laoigh
Crianlarich Jc.
WOOD TERMINAL
CRIANLARICH

F

Loch Awe
Port Sonachan
Glen Falloch
ARDLUI

A R G Y L L
Ben Vorlich
Ben Vane
Loch Lomond

G

ARROCHAR & TARBET
Ben Lomond

Thirty three

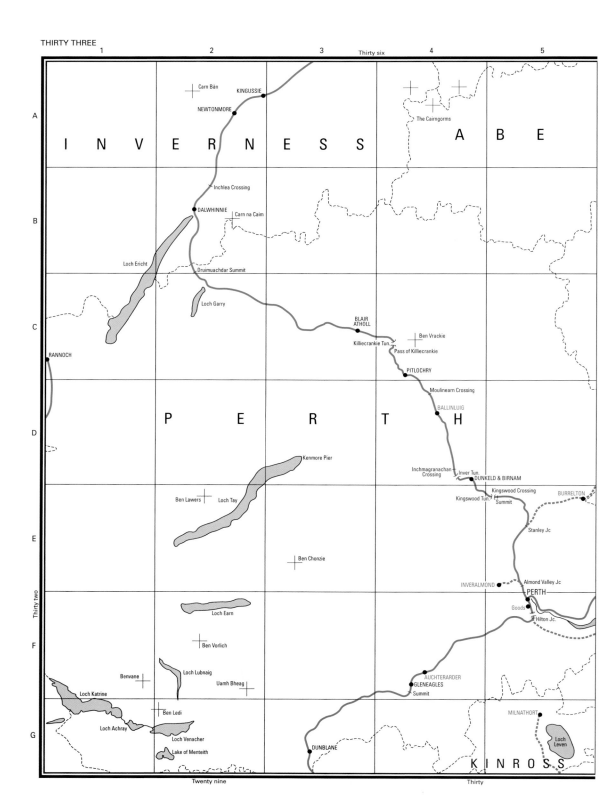

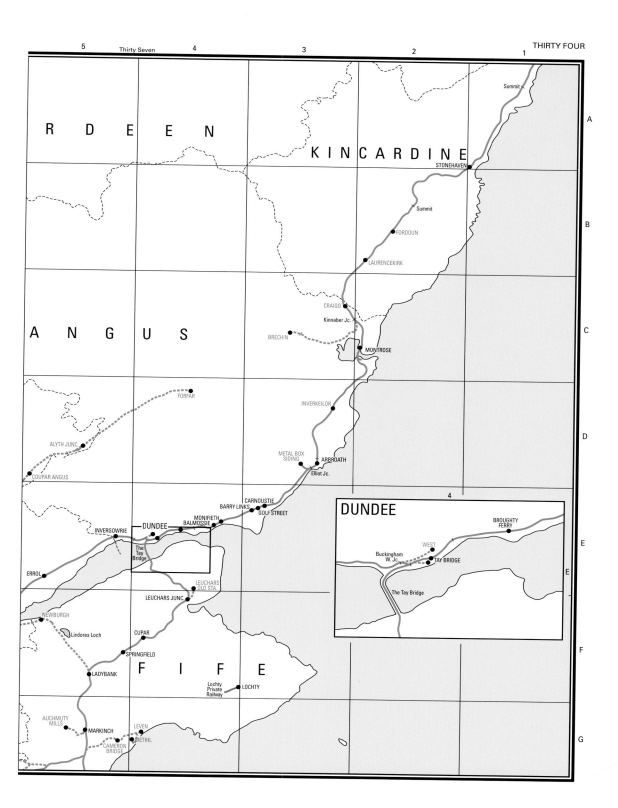

A

R D E E N

KINCARDINE

Summit

STONEHAVEN

B

Summit

FORDOUN

LAURENCEKIRK

A N G U S

CRAIGO

Kinnaber Jc.

C

BRECHIN

MONTROSE

FORFAR

INVERKEILOR

D

ALYTH JUNC.

COUPAR ANGUS

METAL BOX
SIDING   ARBROATH

Elliot Jc.

CARNOUSTIE

BARRY LINKS   GOLF STREET

INVERGOWRIE   DUNDEE   MONIFIETH
BALMOSSIE

The
Tay
Bridge

ERROL

LEUCHARS
OLD STA.

LEUCHARS JUNC.

NEWBURGH

Lindores Loch

CUPAR

SPRINGFIELD

F I F E

LADYBANK

Lochty
Private
Railway   LOCHTY

AUCHMUTY
MILLS

MARKINCH   LEVEN
METHIL

CAMERON
BRIDGE

E

4

DUNDEE

BROUGHTY
FERRY

WEST

Buckingham
W. Jc.   TAY BRIDGE

The Tay Bridge

E

E

F

G

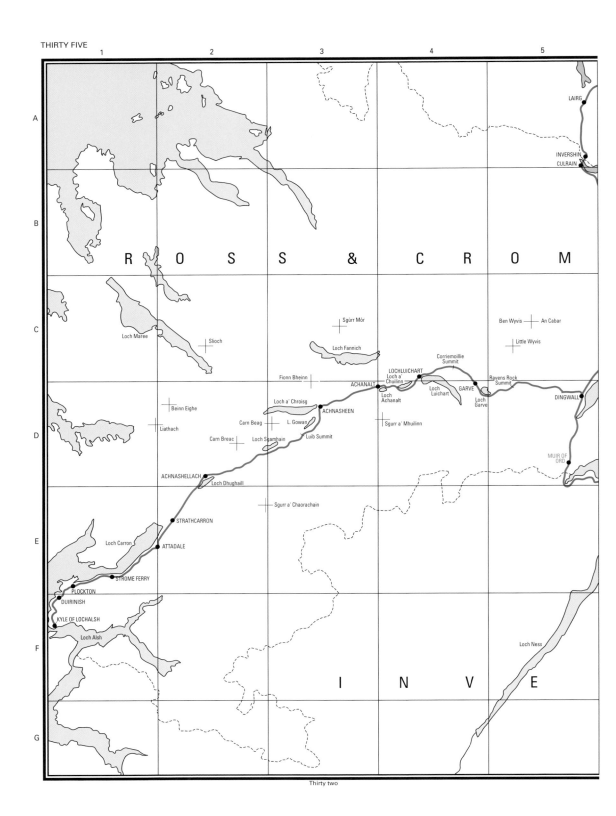

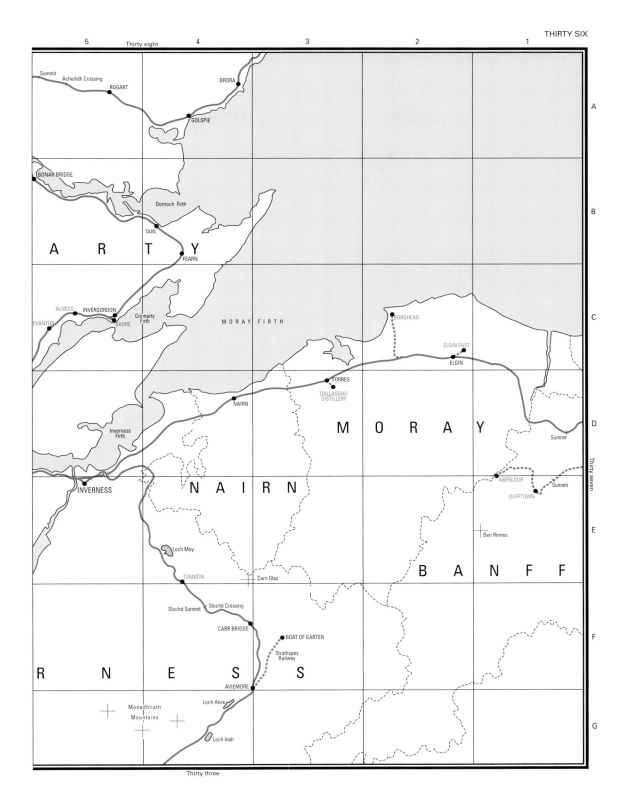

5 Thirty eight 4 3 2 1

Summit
Acheilidh Crossing
ROGART
BRORA
GOLSPIE

A

BONAR BRIDGE

Dornoch Firth

B

TAIN

A R T Y
FEARN

ALNESS INVERGORDON
EVANTON SHORE
Cromarty Firth
MORAY FIRTH
BURGHEAD
ELGIN EAST
ELGIN

C

FORRES
DALLASDHU DISTILLERY
NAIRN

Inverness Firth

M O R A Y
Summit

D

INVERNESS

N A I R N
ABERLOUR
Summit
DUFFTOWN

Thirty seven

Ben Rinnes

E

Loch Moy

TOMATIN
Carn Glas

B A N F F

Slochd Summit Slochd Crossing
CARR BRIDGE
BOAT OF GARTEN
Strathspey Railway

F

R N E S S
AVIEMORE

Loch Alvie

Monadhliath Mountains

Loch Insh

G

Thirty three

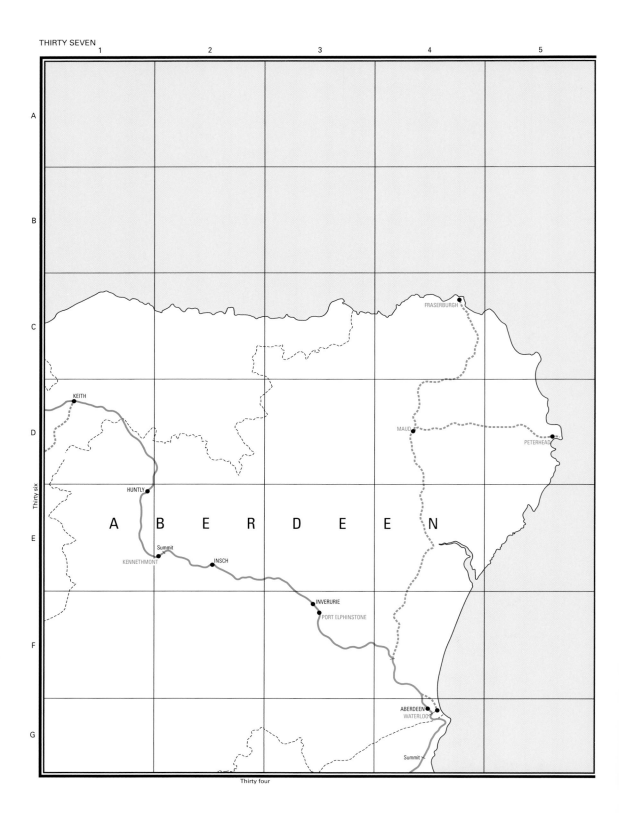

1 2 3 4 5

A

B

C

FRASERBURGH

D

KEITH

MAUD

PETERHEAD

HUNTLY

Thirty six

A B E R D E E N

Summit

KENNETHMONT INSCH

INVERURIE

PORT ELPHINSTONE

ABERDEEN
WATERLOO

Summit

G

Thirty four

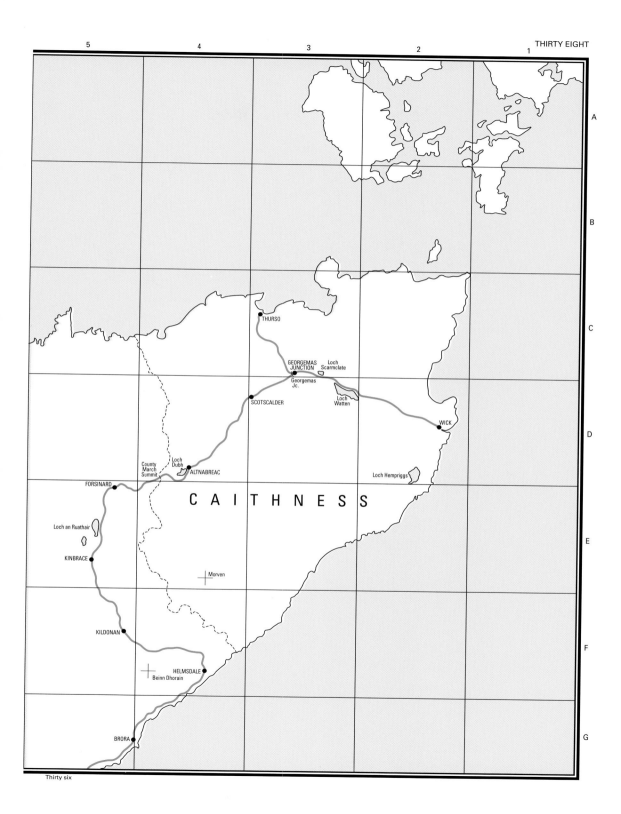

THURSO

GEORGEMAS
JUNCTION

Loch
Scarmclate

Georgemas
Jc.

SCOTSCALDER

Loch
Watten

WICK

County
March
Summit

Loch
Dubh

ALTNABREAC

Loch Hempriggs

FORSINARD

Loch an Ruathair

C A I T H N E S S

KINBRACE

Morven

KILDONAN

HELMSDALE
Beinn Dhorain

BRORA

1   2   3   4   5

Legend:

1 Gas Factory Jc.
2 Bow Junction
3 Borough Market Jc.
4 CAMDEN ROAD
5 Victoria Park Jc.
6 ALDGATE EAST
7 Millwall Junction
8 Harringay W. Jc.
9 Primrose Hill Tuns
10 WEST HAMPSTEAD
11 St. John's Wood Tun.
12 Hampstead Tun
13 MANSION HOUSE
14 CANNON STREET
15 MONUMENT
16 TOWER HILL
17 Metropolitan Jc.
18 Storey Street Jc.
19 Greenford East Jc.
20 Earls Court Jc.
21 Goods Yard Jc.
22 West London Ext. Jc.
23 KEN. LILLIE BRI. (Sidings)
24 TURNHAM GREEN
25 CHISWICK PARK
26 WEST END LANE
27 LADBROKE GROVE
28 WESTBOURNE PARK
29 ROYAL OAK
30 Junction Rd Jc.
31 KENTISH TOWN WEST
32 PRIMROSE HILL
38 EMBANKMENT

Row A:
HEADSTONE LANE, PINNER, HARROW & WEALDSTONE, QUEENSBURY, KINGSBURY, KENTON, NORTHWICK PARK, PRESTON ROAD, HENDON, HENDON CENTRAL, BRENT CROSS, FINCHLEY CENTRAL, EAST FINCHLEY, Depot

Row B:
NORTH HARROW, WEST HARROW, RAYNER'S LANE, EASTCOTE, SOUTH HARROW, HARROW-ON-THE-HILL, North Jc., South Jc., SOUTH KENTON, NORTH WEMBLEY, SUDBURY HILL HARROW, SUDBURY & HARROW RD., WEMBLEY PARK, WEMBLEY HILL, WEMBLEY CENTRAL, Neasden S. Jc., NEASDEN, DOLLIS HILL, Goods, Pass, STONEBRIDGE PARK, Neasden Jc., WILLESDEN GREEN, BRONDESBURY, WEST HAMPSTEAD MIDLAND, KILBURN, Dudding Hill Jct, Cricklewood Grove Jct., CRICKLEWOOD, FINCHLEY RD & FROGNAL, FINCHLEY RD, WEST HAMPSTEAD, Haverstock Hill Tun., GOSPEL OAK, HAMPSTEAD HEATH, Carlton Rd Jc., GOLDERS GREEN, Brent Curve Jct

Row B/C:
RUISLIP, SOUTH RUISLIP, SUDBURY HILL, SUDBURY TOWN, NORTHOLT, GREENFORD, ALPERTON, PERIVALE, BRONDESBURY PARK, KENSAL RISE, Kensal Green Jc., QUEEN'S PARK, SOUTH HAMPSTEAD, KILBURN HIGH ROAD, Gds, Canfield Place, SWISS COTTAGE, 19

Row C:
Portobello Jc., WESTBOURNE PARK, ROYAL OAK, Goods, CASTLE BAR PARK, DRAYTON GREEN, HANGER LANE, PARK ROYAL, NORTH EALING, WEST ACTON, NORTH ACTON, WILLESDEN JUNC., West London Jc., N. & S.W., Old Oak Jc., Acton Wells Jc., Mitre Bri. Jc., Old Oak Common W. Jc., North Pole Jc., KENSAL GREEN, Kensal Green Tuns, Lords Tun., ST. JOHN'S WOOD, GREAT PORTLAND ST., MARYLEBONE, Goods, EDGWARE RD, BAKER STREET, PADDINGTON, BAYSWATER, PADDINGTON, Pass.

Row C/D:
SOUTH GREENFORD, EALING BROADWAY, EALING COMMON, ACTON MAIN LINE, EAST ACTON, ACTON CENTRAL, WEST EALING, HANWELL, SOUTHALL, WHITE CITY, SHEPHERDS BUSH, LATIMER ROAD, NOTTING HILL GATE, HIGH ST KENSINGTON

Row D:
NORTHFIELDS, SOUTH EALING, N. Jc., ACTON TOWN, Bollo Lane Jc., STH. ACTON, Acton Lane Jc., GOLD HAWK RD, STAMFORD BROOK, RAVENSCOURT PARK, H. & C., MET.-DIS., KENSINGTON OLYMPIA, HAMMERSMITH, Studland Rd Jc., BARON'S COURT, WEST KENSINGTON, EARLS COURT, WEST BROMPTON, Cromwell Curve North Jc., GLOUCESTER RD, Cromwell Curve East Jc., STH. KENSINGTON, SLOANE SQUARE, VICTORIA

Row D:
HOUNSLOW WEST, HOUNSLOW CENTRAL, HOUNSLOW EAST, OSTERLEY, BOSTON MANOR, BRENTFORD CENTRAL, Brentford Lane Jc., GUNNERSBURY, Brentford Jc., KEW BRIDGE, East Jc., New, CHISWICK, KEW GARDENS, BARNES BRIDGE, FULHAM BROADWAY, PARSONS GREEN, Chelsea Basin Jc., Chelsea Basin, Battersea Wharf, BATTERSEA PARK, QUEENS ROAD BATTERSEA

Row D/E:
ISLEWORTH, SYON LANE, BRENT FORD TOWN GOODS, NORTH SHEEN, MORTLAKE, BARNES, PUTNEY BRI., PUTNEY, WANDSWORTH TOWN, Latchmere Jc., CLAPHAM JUNCTION, WANDSWORTH COMMON

Row E:
HOUNSLOW, Hounslow Jc., WHITTON, ST. MARGARETS, TWICKENHAM, RICHMOND, Feltham Jc., Whitton Jc., Battersea Pier Jc., Battersea Wharf, BATTERSEA PARK, QUEEN'S RD, SOUTH LAMBETH, EAST PUTNEY, Point Pleasant Jc., SOUTHFIELDS, WIMBLEDON PARK, EARLSFIELD, BALHAM, Balham Jc., SOUTHFIELDS

Clapham Junction inset:
Latchmere S.W. Jc., CLAPHAM JUNCTION, Ludgate Jc., Falcon Jc., Stewarts Lane Jc., STEWARTS LANE, Factory Jc.

Row F:
KEMPTON PARK, HAMPTON, FULWELL, STRAWBERRY HILL, TEDDINGTON, KINGSTON, NORBITON, HAMPTON WICK, NEW MALDEN, WIMBLEDON, Gds, HAYDONS RD, TOOTING, WIMBLEDON CHASE, RAYNES PARK, MERTON PARK, MERTON ABBEY, SOUTH MERTON, MORDEN ROAD, MITCHAM

Row G:
ESHER, THAMES DITTON, HAMPTON COURT, SURBITON, Hampton Court Jc., BERRYLANDS, MALDEN MANOR, WORCESTER PARK, MOTSPUR PARK, SOUTH MERTON, MORDEN SOUTH, ST HELIER, MITCHAM JUNC., HACKBRIDGE

5 4 3 2 1

GREATER LONDON

NEW SOUTHGATE & FRIERN BARNET
SILVER STREET FOR UPPER EDMONTON
BOWES PARK
WHITE HART LANE
NORTHUMBERLAND PARK
WOOD STREET
SOUTH WOODFORD
FAIRLOP

A

WOOD GREEN (ALEXANDRA PARK)
BRUCE GROVE
TOTTENHAM HALE
N. Jc.
W. Jc.
S. Jc.
WALTHAMSTOW CENTRAL
SNARESBROOK
Primrose Hill
Hampstead Rd Jc.
BARKING-SIDE
HORNSEY
BLACK HORSE RD
WALTHAMSTOW QUEENS ROAD
Primrose Hill Jc.
NEWBURY PARK
HARRINGAY WEST
SEVEN SISTERS
SOUTH TOTTENHAM
South Tottenham Jc.
ST JAMES' STR
CROUCH HILL
HARRINGAY STADIUM
STAMFORD HILL
Copper Mill Jc.
LEYTONSTONE

UPPER HOLLOWAY
30
FINSBURY PARK
STOKE NEWINGTON
Clapton Jc.
LEA BRIDGE
LEYTON MIDLAND ROAD
LEYTONSTONE HIGH ROAD
MANOR PARK
ILFORD

B

31
KENTISH TOWN
RECTORY ROAD
CLAPTON
LEYTON
WANSTEAD PARK
FOREST GATE
Forest Gate Jc.
WOODGRANGE PARK
Barking East Jc.
CANONBURY
Western Jc.
HACKNEY DOWNS
Temple Mills East Jc.
FOREST GATE
EAST HAM LOOP NTH Jc.
BARKING
Canonbury Jc.
HIGHBURY & ISLINGTON
CALEDONIAN ROAD & BARNSBURY
DALSTON JUNC.
LONDON FIELDS
MARY LAND Goods
STRATFORD LOWER
EAST HAM
EAST HAM BOROUGH COUNCIL SIDING
Gasworks Tun.
Street Factory Jc.
STRATFORD MARKET
HAMPSTEAD HEATH
Junction Rd Jc.
YORK ROAD
ST PANCRAS
KING'S CROSS
G.N. Gds Jc.
FARRINGDON
CAMBRIDGE HEATH
BETHNAL GREEN
UPTON PARK
PLAISTOW
GOSPEL OAK
Carlton Rd Jc.
Kentish Town Jc.

C

EUSTON
KING'S CROSS (LT.)
BARBICAN
MOORGATE
E. Jc.
BOW ROAD
MILE END
WEST HAM
KENTISH TOWN WEST
KENTISH TOWN
EUSTON SQUARE
LIV. ST MET.
BROAD STREET
SHOREDITCH
STEPNEY GREEN
BROMLEY BY BOW
PLAISTOW & WEST HAM
HOLBORN VIADUCT
LIVERPOOL STREET
WHITECHAPEL
CANNING TOWN NORTH
BECKTON
FENCHURCH STREET
ALDGATE
SHADWELL
CANNING TOWN
BLACKFRIARS
TEMPLE
WAPPING
STEPNEY EAST
CUSTOM HOUSE VICTORIA DOCK
CHARING CROSS
MET-DIS
WESTMINSTER
WATERLOO EAST
SILVERTOWN
NORTH WOOLWICH
ABBEY WOOD

D

ST JAMES' PARK
WATERLOO
LONDON BRIDGE
ROTHERHITHE
ANGERSTEIN WHARF
PLUMSTEAD
VAUXHALL
ELEPHANT & CASTLE
BRICKLAYERS ARMS
SURREY DOCKS
MILLWALL DOCKS
WOOLWICH ARSENAL
North Kent West Jc.
Corbet's Lane Jc.
WESTCOMBE PARK
CHARLTON
WOOLWICH DOCKYARD
SOUTH LAMBETH
SOUTH BERMONDSEY
Surrey Canal Jc.
Nth Kent Jc.
MAZE HILL
Bricklayers Arms Jc.
DEPTFORD
WANDSWORTH ROAD
LOUGHBOROUGH JUNC.
QUEENS ROAD PECKHAM
PECKHAM RYE
Cow Lane Jc.
NUNHEAD
GREENWICH
Canterbury Rd Jc.
Coal
BRIXTON
DENMARK HILL
NEW CROSS
ST JOHN'S
CLAPHAM HIGH STREET
EAST BRIXTON
Cambria Rd Jc.
EAST DULWICH
NEW CROSS GATE
LEWISHAM
FALCONWOOD
WELLING

E

N. Jc.
HERNE HILL
S. Jc.
NORTH DULWICH
BROCKLEY
Parks Bridge Jc.
BLACKHEATH
KIDBROOKE
ELTHAM PARK
STREATHAM HILL
TULSE HILL
WEST DULWICH
HONOR OAK PARK
CROFTON PARK
HITHER GREEN
Lee Jc.
LEE
ELTHAM WELL HALL
LADYWELL
FOREST HILL
CATFORD BRIDGE
GROVE PARK
NEW ELTHAM
ALBANY PARK
Knights Hill Tun.
Leigham Jc.
CATFORD
MOTTINGHAM
SIDCUP
Streatham N. Jc.
SYDENHAM HILL
West Norwood Jc.
WEST NORWOOD
SYDENHAM
Leigham Tuns.

F

Streatham Tun.
STREATHAM
GIPSY HILL
Penge Tun.
BELLINGHAM
LOWER SYDENHAM
Streatham S.Jc.
STREATHAM COMMON
PENGE EAST
BECKENHAM HILL
Chislehurst Tun.
ELMSTEAD WOODS
Streatham Jc.
CRYSTAL PALACE
PENGE WEST
KENT HOUSE
NEW BECKENHAM
RAVENSBOURNE
SUNDRIDGE PARK
NORBURY
ANERLEY
New Beckenham Jc.
Penge Jc.
BECKENHAM JUNC.
CHISLEHURST
Chislehurst Jc.
Bromley Jc.
Shortlands Jc.
THORNTON HEATH
SELHURST
Spur Jc. BIRKBECK
CLOCK HOUSE
SHORTLANDS
BROMLEY NORTH
Bickley Jc.
St Mary Cray Jc.
NORWOOD JUNC.
ELMERS END
BROMLEY SOUTH
BICKLEY
ST MARY CRAY
Selhurst Jc.
Petts Wood Jc.

G

BEDDINGTON LANE
Gloucester Rd Jc.
EDEN PARK
PETTS WOOD
WADDON MARSH
WEST CROYDON
WOODSIDE
Woodside Jc.
Windmill Bridge Jc.
ADDISCOMBE
WEST WICKHAM
HAYES
ORPINGTON

1   2   3   4   5

DERBY & NOTTINGHAM TO SHEFFIELD

SHEFFIELD
Woodburn Jc.
DARNALL
NUNNERY
L.S.
Treeton Jc.
THURCROFT
Dinnington Colliery
Laughton E. Jc.
Dinnington Jc.
WOODHOUSE
BEIGHTON
KIVETON BRIDGE
KIVETON PARK
Brancliffe Jc.
W. Jc.
E. Jc.
SHIREOAKS
S. Jc.
WORKSOP
MILLHOUSES & ECCLESALL
STEETLEY

A

DORE & TOTLEY
Bradway Tun.
SPINKHILL
WHITWELL
MANTON WOOD
Totley Tun.
GRINDLEFORD

B

SHEEPBRIDGE IRON WORKS
Broomhouse Tun.
BARROW HILL
CRESWELL
SHEEPBRIDGE
Tapton Jc.
CHESTERFIELD
MARKHAM
WELBECK
ARKWRIGHT TOWN
BOLSOVER
LANGWITH

C

SHIREBROOK
WARSOP
THORESBY
Clipstone Jc.
GLAPWELL COLLIERY
PLEASLEY WEST
CLIPSTONE
Clay Cross Tun.
CLAY CROSS
TEVERSALL
SHERWOOD
MANSFIELD
RUFFORD
BILSTHORPE

D

MATLOCK
High Tor Tuns.
DOE HILL
TIBSHELF & NEWTON
SUTTON
SUTTON-IN-ASHFIELD
Willersley Tun.
NEW HUCKNALL
CROMFORD
WESTHOUSES
Lea Wood Tun.
Alfreton Tun.
PINXTON NORTH
BLIDWORTH
WIRKSWORTH
WHATSTANDWELL
Wingfield Tun.
BENTINCK
ANNESLEY

E

Pye Bridge Jc.
BUTTERLEY
LINBY
AMBERGATE
CODNOR PARK
HUCKNALL
S. Jc.
CALVERTON
BELPER
DENBY
BESTWOOD

F

MOOR GREEN
Milford Tun.
DUFFIELD
BABBINGTON
BURTON JOYCE
GEDLING
CARLTON & NETHERFIELD FOR GEDLING & COLWICK
Little Eaton Jc.
WEST HALLAM
Weekday Cross Jc.
NETHERFIELD & COLWICK
Gds
COLWICK
NOTTINGHAM

G

FRIARGATE
STANTON GATE
BEESTON
EDWALTON
COTGRAVE
MICKLEOVER
DERBY
ST ANDREWS
Chaddesden Sidings
SPONDON
ATTENBOROUGH
Toton Marshalling Yard
RUDDINGTON

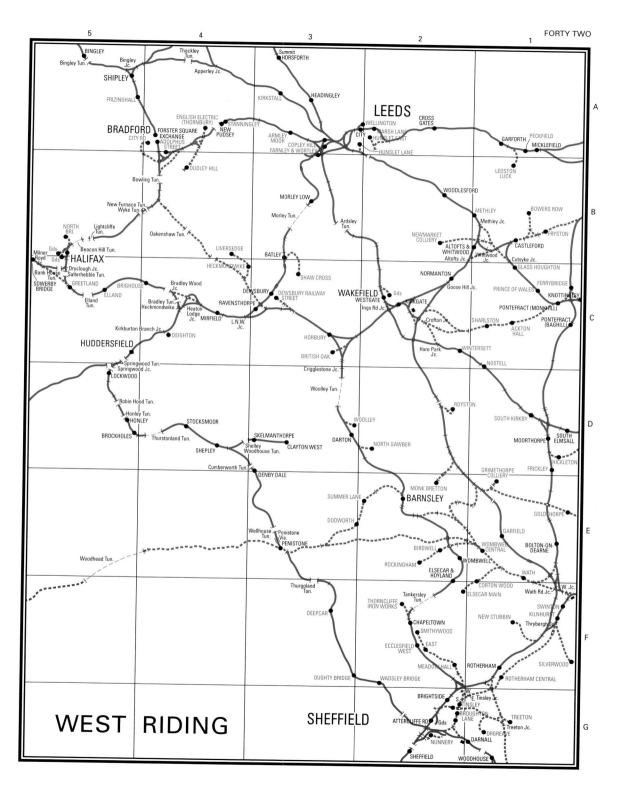

5   4   3   2   1

A
B
C
D
E
F
G

BINGLEY
Bingley Tun.
Bingley Jc.
Thackley Tun.
SHIPLEY
Apperley Jc.
Summit
HORSFORTH
FRIZINGHALL
KIRKSTALL
HEADINGLEY
LEEDS
ENGLISH ELECTRIC (THORNBURY)
STANNINGLEY
WELLINGTON
CROSS GATES
BRADFORD
FORSTER SQUARE
EXCHANGE
NEW PUDSEY
MARSH LANE
HUNSLET EAST
GARFORTH
PECKFIELD
CITY RD
ADOLPHUS STREET
ARMLEY MOOR
COPLEY HILL
CITY
MICKLEFIELD
FARNLEY & WORTLEY
HUNSLET LANE
DUDLEY HILL
LEDSTON LUCK
Bowling Tun.
WOODLESFORD
New Furnace Tun.
Wyke Tun.
MORLEY LOW
METHLEY
BOWERS ROW
NORTH BRI.
Lightcliffe Tun.
Morley Low
Ardsley Tun.
Methley Jc.
FRYSTON
Oakenshaw Tun.
NEWMARKET COLLIERY
ALTOFTS & WHITWOOD
CASTLEFORD
Milner Royd Gds
LIVERSEDGE
Altofts Jc.
Whitwood Jc.
Cutsyke Jc.
GLASS HOUGHTON
HALIFAX
Beacon Hill Tun.
BATLEY
HECKMONDWIKE
SHAW CROSS
NORMANTON
FERRYBRIDGE
Bank House Tun.
Dryclough Jc.
Salterhebble Tun.
Bradley Wood Jc.
DEWSBURY
Goose Hill Jc.
PRINCE OF WALES
KNOTTINGLEY
SOWERBY BRIDGE
GREETLAND
BRIGHOUSE
DEWSBURY RAILWAY STREET
WAKEFIELD
WESTGATE
Gds
Elland Tun.
ELLAND
Bradley Tun.
Heckmondwike Jc.
RAVENSTHORPE
PONTEFRACT (MONKHILL)
Kirkburton Branch Jc.
Heaton Lodge Jc.
MIRFIELD
L.N.W. Jc.
Ings Rd Jc.
KIRKGATE
SHARLSTON
PONTEFRACT (BAGHILL)
HUDDERSFIELD
DEIGHTON
Crofton Jc.
ACKTON HALL
HORBURY
Hare Park Jc.
WINTERSETT
Springwood Tun.
Springwood Jc.
BRITISH OAK
NOSTELL
LOCKWOOD
Crigglestone Jc.
Woolley Tun.
Robin Hood Tun.
ROYSTON
Honley Tun.
STOCKSMOOR
WOOLLEY
SOUTH KIRKBY
HONLEY
SKELMANTHORPE
DARTON
NORTH GAWBER
MOORTHORPE
SOUTH ELMSALL
BROCKHOLES
Thurstonland Tun.
SHELLEY
Woodhouse Tun.
CLAYTON WEST
HICKLETON
SHEPLEY
Cumberworth Tun.
GRIMETHORPE COLLIERY
FRICKLEY
DENBY DALE
MONK BRETTON
GOLDTHORPE
SUMMER LANE
BARNSLEY
DODWORTH
DARFIELD
Wellhouse Tun.
Penistone Via.
BIRDWELL
WOMBWELL CENTRAL
BOLTON-ON-DEARNE
Woodhead Tun.
PENISTONE
ROCKINGHAM
WOMBWELL
WATH
Thurgoland Tun.
CORTON WOOD
Wath Rd Jc.
W. Jc.
Tankersley Tun.
ELSECAR MAIN
SWINTON
DEEPCAR
THORNCLIFFE IRON WORKS
ELSECAR & HOYLAND
NEW STUBBIN
KILNHURST
CHAPELTOWN
Thrybergh Jc.
SMITHYWOOD
ECCLESFIELD WEST
EAST
MEADOW HALL
SILVERWOOD
OUGHTY BRIDGE
WADSLEY BRIDGE
ROTHERHAM
ROTHERHAM CENTRAL
BRIGHTSIDE
W.
S.
E. Tinsley Jc.
TINSLEY
ATTERCLIFFE RD
Gds
BROUGHTON LANE
TREETON
Treeton Jc.
NUNNERY
DARNALL
ORGREAVE
SHEFFIELD
WOODHOUSE

WEST RIDING

SHEFFIELD

SOUTH WALES

1 2 3 4 5

A B C D E F G

ABERGAVENNY
ABERGAVENNY (BRECON RD)
Sugar Loaf
BLAENAVON
GLASCOED
PONTYPOOL ROAD
HAFODYRYNYS
West Maindee Jc.
North DOCK STR.
Pillbank
USKMOUTH
NEWPORT
Llantarnam Jc.
ROGERSTONE
Gaer Jcs.
Park Jcs.
Alexandra Dock
Ebbw Jc.
ROSE HEYWORTH
SIX BELLS
BLAINA
MARINE
MARKHAM
CELYNEN NORTH
CELYNEN SOUTH
EBBW VALE
BARGOED
OAKDALE
Hall's Tramway Jc.
Risca Jc.
MACHEN
BIRD-IN-HAND
LLANBRADACH
BEDWAS
ABER
Aber Branch Jc.
CAERPHILLY
Caerphilly Tun.
LLANISHEN
HEATH HL
Heath Jc.
Heath Half Jc.
PENARTH DOCK
DINGLE ROAD
PENARTH
BRAITH COL & MILEAGE DEPOT
Splott Jc.
GRANGE TOWN
CARDIFF
CADOXTON
BARRY PIER
BARRY ISLAND
BARRY
BARRY DOCKS
COGAN
DINAS POWIS
PONTLOTTYN
TIR PHIL
Deri Jc.
McCLAREN
BRITHDIR
TAFF MERTHYR & TRELEWIS
DEEP NAVIGATION
PENALLTA
HENGOED
Penallta Branch Jc.
YSTRAD MYNACH
WINDSOR COLLIERY
NANTGARW COLLIERY
TAFF WELL
CORYTON
RHIWBINA
WHITCHURCH
RADYR
Penarth Curve Jcs.
Penarth Bch. Jc.
LLANDAFF FOR WHITCHURCH
RHYMNEY
CWM BARGOED
DOWLAIS
MERTHYR
PENTREBACH
TROEDYRHIW
MERTHYR VALE
NEW TOWN
QUAKERS YARD
MOUNTAIN ASH
ABERCYNON
LADY WINDSOR
TREHAFOD
PONTYPRIDD
PENRHIWCEIBER
CREIGIAU QUARRY
Cannon Bch. Jc.
CWM
LLANTRISANT
Mwyndy Jc.
LLANHARRY
PENDERYN
ABERDARE
MAERDY
BLAENRHONDDA
TREHERBERT
Blaenrhondda Tun.
TREORCHY
YSTRAD (RHONDDA)
BLAENGWYNFI
LLWYNYPIA
TONYPANDY & TREALAW
WYNDHAM
OGMORE
DINAS (RHONDDA)
PORTH
COED ELY
RAGLAN
LLANHARAN
Y Fan gihirach
TOWER
CRAIG-Y-NOS
CWMMER AFAN
CAERAU
PONTYCYMMER
GARTH
PONTYRHYL
LLANGEINOR
BLAENGARW
CWMDU
TONDU
Coity Jc.
COITY
BRIDGEND
ONLLWYN
GLYN NEATH
ABERPERGWM
YNYSARWED
BLAENANT
GLYNCORRWG
NANTY FFYLLON
MAESTEG
TROEDYRHEW
GARTH
LLANGYNWYD
MARGAM GOODS & COAL DEPOT
Margam Jc.
MILL PIT
Cefn Jc.
Pyle Jc.
PORT TALBOT
Docks
PANTYFFYNNON
AMMANFORD & TIRYDAIL
AMMANFORD Jc.
Pantyffynnon Jc.
GWAUN-CAE-GURWEN
ABERNANT
CLYDACH ON TAVE NORTH
NEATH ABBEY
NEATH
Neath Jc.
Cardonnel Jc.
Court Sart Jc.
BRITON FERRY
JERSEY MARINE
BAGLAN BAY
DANYGRAIG SIDING
LLANDEBIE
CRAIG MERTHYR
VELINDRE
Llangyfelach Tun.
MORRISTON EAST
Pantlergaer Tun.
UPPER BANK
E. Jc.
SWANSEA
CADOXTON
DANYGRAIG

1 CARDIFF QUEEN ST
2 CARDIFF GENERAL
3 TREFOREST ESTATE
4 CEFN ON
5 GLYN ON FARGOED
6 HEATH HALT LL
7 BIRCH GROVE
8 CARDIFF BUTE ROAD

GLASGOW & DISTRICT

CUMBERNAULD
GARTSHORE
MILNGAVIE
HILLFOOT
BEARSDEN
KILPATRICK
OLD KILPATRICK
DALMUIR PARK
DALMUIR RIVERSIDE
SINGER
DRUMRY
CLYDEBANK
DRUMCHAPEL
YOKER
GARSCADDEN
SCOTSTOUNHILL
JORDANHILL
HYNDLAND
HYNDLAND
ANNIESLAND
Knightswood Nth. Jc.
Mingavie Jc.
WESTERTON
LOCHBURN
LENZIE
CADDER YARD
BISHOPBRIGGS
POSSIL PARK
PARTICK HILL
MILLERSTON
STEPPS
BEDLAY COLLIERY
GARTCOSH
Gartcosh Jc.
Garnqueen N. Jc.
Garnqueen S. Jc.
COATDYKE
SUN FOUNDRY
Greenside Jc.
SUNNYSIDE
ARDRIE
CENTRAL
COATBRIDGE
CANAL
CALDER
BLAIRHILL
EASTERHOUSE
GARROWHILL
SHETTLESTON
CARNTYNE
SIGHTHILL
BRIDGETON
CARMYLE
LONDON ROAD
RUTHERGLEN
SPRINGBURN
RENFREW
PAISLEY
ST. JAMES
GILMOUR STREET
CANAL
FERGUSLIE
DEANSIDE TRANSIT DEPOT
SOUTH SHIELDS
RENFREW WHARF
CARDONALD
MOSSPARK WEST
CORKERHILL
HILLINGTON WEST
HILLINGTON EAST
HAWKHEAD
CROOKSTON
Amfleton Jc.
Wallneuk Jc.
Walkinshaw Pch. Jc.
DINWOOD DEPOT
LINWOOD MINERAL
GENERAL TERMINUS
MAXWELL PARK
POLLOKSHIELDS W.
CROSSMYLOOF
POLLOKSHAWS EAST
POLLOKSHAWS WEST
LANGSIDE
Busby Jc.
SHAWLANDS
CATHCART
MOUNT FLORIDA
KINGS PARK
CROFTFOOT
CAMBUSLANG
KIRKHILL
Kirkhill Jc.
BURNSIDE
Kirkhill Jc.
Rutherglen Jc.
E. Jc.
QUEENS PARK
P'SHIELDS E.
CROSSHILL
KENNISHEAD
NITSHILL
THORNLIEBANK
GIFFNOCK
MUIREND
WILLIAMWOOD
WHITECRAIGS
PATTERTON
CLARKSTON & STAMPERLAND
BUSBY
THORNTONHALL
HAIRMYRES
EAST KILBRIDE
BRIDGETON
NEILSTON
BARRHEAD
BELLAHOUSTON
GENERAL TERMINUS
POLLOKSHIELDS WEST
POLLOKSHIELDS EAST
Langside Jc.
Muirhouse South. Jc.
Terminus Jc.
HIGH STREET
CENTRAL
CLELAND
WISHAW
WISHAW (SOUTH)
N. Jc.
Shielmuir Jc.
Dalzell Jc.
CARFIN
HOLYTOWN
Fullwood Jcs.
MOSSEND
S. Jc.
Roods
FLEMINGTON
BSC TIP
Ross Jc.
MOTHERWELL
Lesmahagow Jc.
HAMILTON WEST
HAMILTON CEN.
BELLSHILL
N. Jc.
BLANTYRE
Uddingston Jc.
UDDINGSTON
Newton Jc.
NEWTON
N. Jc.

1 CHARING CROSS
2 CENTRAL
3 QUEEN STREET
4 Shields Jc.
5 Bridge Street Jc.
6 Eglinton Street Jc.
7 SPRINGBURN
8 BARNHILL
9 Gorbals Jc.
10 BELLGROVE
11 DUKE STREET
12 ALEXANDRA PARADE
13 Larkfield Jc.
14 ST. ROLLOX WORKS

LIVERPOOL & MANCHESTER

1 WARWICK ROAD for OLD TRAFFORD
2 BRADLEY FOLD for LITTLE LEVER
3 NEW BRIGHTON
4 WALLASEY GROVE ROAD
5 WALLASEY VILLAGE
6 HAMILTON SQUARE
7 BIRKENHEAD PARK
8 VAUXHALL JUNCTION
9 ASHTON-IN-MAKERFIELD
10 BANK HALL
11 MANCHESTER PICCADILLY
12 LIVERPOOL EXCHANGE
13 BIRKENHEAD NORTH
14 FARNWORTH 7 HALSHAW MOOR
15 MOORSIDE & WARDLEY
16 JAMES STREET
17 LIVERPOOL CENTRAL
18 WOODLANDS RD
19 GREENHUME
20 EDGE HILL
21 DEANSGATE
22 MANCHESTER DOCKS STA.
23 CROWN STREET
24 EDGE HILL
25 MANCHESTER VICTORIA
26 CANADA DOCK
27 OLDHAM RD
28 ALEXANDRA & WELLINGTON DOCK
29 MANCHESTER) OXFORD ROAD
30 ANCOATS
31 BOOTLE ORIEL ROAD
32 NEW STRAND
33 MAYFIELD
34 KIRKDALE
35 BENTLE BRIDGE
36 RHODE BRIDGE
37 HEATON NORRIS
38 SANDHILLS
39 SEACOMBE
40 LIVERPOOL ROAD
41 CHESSINGTON & GRASSENDALE

MANCHESTER

LIVERPOOL

SOUTHPORT

BOLTON

BURY

ROCHDALE

OLDHAM

STOCKPORT

MACCLESFIELD

WARRINGTON

WIGAN

ST HELENS

BIRKENHEAD

GARSTON

RUNCORN

Name	Ref	Name	Ref	Name	Ref	Name	Ref
Cowie	30B5	Dunston on Tyne	28B2	Fowey	1D3	Hemelite Works	11F1
Coxlodge	27B5	Dursley	8B1/9F2	Fraserburgh	37C4	Hemyock	2A2/8G4
Craft	16F4	Dysart	30A2	Fremington Quay	7F3	Herbrandston	77D1
Craig Merthyr	43G2	Dyserth	19C5	Frickley	21F4/42D1	Hereford Moorfields	9C1
Craig-y-Nos	7A5/43E1			Frizinghall	21D2/42A5	Hethersett	18F3
Craigo	34C3	Easington	28D5	Frosterley	27D4	Hetton	28D5
Cranmore	3C3/8E1	East Cauldedown	1D2	Fryston	21E4/42B1	Hickleton	21F4/42D1
Creigiau Quarry	43C4	East Ham Borough Council				High Marnham	16B2
Cresswell	16A4/41B4	Siding	40B2	Gartcosh	44C4	Highgate	5A3
Crianlarich Wood		East Hetton	28D5	Gartshore	44B5	Hindlow	15B5
Terminal	33F1	East Leake	16D4	Gasswater	29E5	Holditch	15C3/20E1
Crombie	30B3	Eastgate	27D3	Gedling	16C3/41F5	Hollins	20A2
Cronton	45E4	Easton	30C4	General Terminus (Glasgow)		Holme	11A2/17G2
Crown Street	45F3	Easton Lodge	11E4		44E3	Holwell	16E3
Croxley Mill	11G1	Eastriggs	26B2	Giffen	29D3	Holywell Junction	20D5
Curzon Street	13C4	Ebbw Vale	8A4/43B1	Glapwell Colliery	16B4/41C3	Horbury	21E3/42C3
Cuxhoe	28D5	Eccles	28B5	Glascoed	8B3/43A2	Horncastle	17B2
Cwm	43C4	Ecclesfield	21G3/42F2	Glasshoughton	42C1	Horrocksford	24D1
Cwm Bargoed	43C2	Ecclesfield East	42F2	Glaxo Works	24B4	Horsehay & Dawley	15F2
Cwm Mawr	7A3	Edge Hill	45F4	Glen Garnock BSC	29D3	Horwich	20B2/24F2/45C1
Cwmdu	7B5/43E3	Edwalton	16D3/41G5	Glyn Neath	7A5/43E2	Hotchley	16E5
Cynheidre	7A3	Egremont	26F3	Glyncorrwg	7B5/43E2	Hotchley Hill	16D4
		Eldon Street	28A1	Goldington	11D1	Hownes Gill	27C5
Dallasdhu	36D3	Elgin East	36C2	Goldthorpe	42E1	Hucknall	16C4/41E4
Dalmuir Riverside	44G5	Elland	21E2/42C5	Goole Docks	22E5	Hugglescote	16E4
Dan-y-Craig	7B4/43F3	Elsecar Main	42F2	Goonerby Siding	16D1	Humberstone Road	16F3
Darfield	21F4/42E1	Elswick	28A2	Gorseinon	7B3	Hunslet East	21D3/42A2
Deanside Transit Depot	44F4	Elvington	21C5	Gosford Green	10A5	Hunslet Lane	42A3
Deep Navigation	43C2	Enderby	16F4	Grain	6B4	Huskisson	45F4
Deepcar	21F3/42F3	English Electric		Grangemouth	30B4	Hylton	28C5
Deepdale	24D3	(Thornbury)	42A4	Granton	30B2	Hyndland	44E4
Deighton	21E2/42C4	Eskmeals	26G3	Granville	15E2		
Denby	16C5/41F2	Etherley	27E5	Great Bridge North	13A2	Immingham	22E3
Derby Friargate	16D5/41G2	Evanton	36C5	Great Mountain	7A3	Immingham Docks	22E2
Derby St Andrews	16D5/41G2			Greetland	21E2/42C5	Inveralmond	33E5
Dereham	18E4	Fakenham	18D5	Grimethorpe	21F4/42E1	Invergordon Shore	36C5
Derwenthaugh	28A3	Fallowfield	20C1/24G1/45A3	Grimsargh	24D2	Inverkeilor	34D3
Desford	16F4	Farnley & Wortley	42A3	Grimsby Docks	22F2	Ironbridge	15F2
Dewsbury Railway Street	42C3	Farnworth & Bold	15A1/45D$	Gunness	22F5	Irvine Goods	29E3
Dinnington	16A4/41A4	Faversham Docks	6C3	Gwaun Cae Gurwen	7A4/43F1	Irvine Harbour	29E3
Dinton	3C5	Fawley	4E4			Islip	10A1
Dodworth	21F3/42E3	Felin Fach	13E5	Hafodyrnys	8B4/43A2	Ivybridge	2D5
Doe Hill	16B4/41D3	Felsted	11E5	Halifax North Bridge	21E2/42B5		
Dollar	30A4	Ferguslie	44G3	Halliwell	20B2/24F2/45C2	Jersey Marine	7B4/43F3
Donisthorpe	16E5	Ferrybridge	21E4/42C1	Hamilton BSC Tip	44B2		
Donnington	15E2	Ferryhiill	28D5	Hamworthy	3F5	Keadby	22F4
Dowlais Top	8A5/43C2	Fiddlers Ferry & Penketh		Harlaxton	16D2	Keighley South	21D1
Dowver Town Yard	6D2		15A1/20C3/24G3/45D4	Harpur Hill	15B4	Kelty	30A3
Drax	21E5	Finchley Road	39B5	Hartlepool	28D4	Kennethmont	37E2
Drayton	4E1/5F1	Fishburn	28D5	Hartley	28B5	Kensington Lillie Bridge	39D4
Drinnick Mill	1D2	Fisherrow	30B2	Harworth	21G5	Keresley	16G5
Drongan	29F4	Fishguard & Goodwick	13F1	Haswell	28D5	Ketton	16F1
Dudley	13B1/15G4	Flemington	30C5/44A2	Havannah	27B5	Killamarsh	16A4
Dudley	27B5	Fletton	11A2/17G2	Haverton Hill	28E4	Killingholme	22E3
Dudley Hill	21D2/42B4	Flixborough	22E5	Hawkesbury	16G5	Killoch Colliery	29F4
Dufftown	36E1	Florence	15C3/20F1	Hawkhead	44F3	Kilnhurst	21F4/42F1
Dumbuck Siding	29B4	Foley Park	9A3	Heap Bridge	20B1/24F1/45A1	Kincardine	30A4
Dundee West	34E4	Forest Gate	40B2	Heathfield	2C4	Kineton	10B5
Dunfermline Upper	30A3	Forfar	34D4	Heaton Norris	45A4	King George Dock	22E3
Dungeness	6E3	Foss Island	21A4	Heckmondwike	42C4	Kingsbury	15F5
Dunnington	21C5	Four Ashes	15E3	Helsby & Alvanley	45E5	Kingsheath	15G4
Dunstable	10D1/11E1	Fourdoun	34B2	Hem Heath	15D3/20F1	Kingshill	30D5

INDEX TO PASSENGER STATIONS

Station	Reference
Kiveton Bridge	16A4/41A4
Kiveton Park	16A4/41A4
Knaresborough	21C3
Knebworth	11E2
Knighton	14D2
Knockholt	5C4
Knottingley for Ferrybridge	21E4
Knucklas	14D2
Knutsford	15A2/20D2/45B5
Kyle of Lochalsh	35F1
Ladbroke Grove	39C4
Lade Halt	6E3
Ladybank	34F5
Ladywell	40E3
Laindon	5A5
Lairg	35A5
Lakenheath	11A5/17G5
Lakeside	24A3/26G1
Lambley	27C2
Lamphey	7D2
Lanark	30D4
Lancaster	24C3
Lancing	5F2
Landywood	15E4
Langbank	29B3
Langley	5B1/10G1
Langley Green	13C2/15G4
Langside	44E3
Langwathby	27D1
Lapford	2A4
Lapworth	9A5
Larbert	30B5
Largs	29C2
Latimer Road	39C4
Lawrence Hill	3A2
Laxey	23B3
Layton	24D4
Lazonby & Kirkoswald	27D1
Lea Bridge	40B3
Lea Hall	15G5
Leagrave	10D1/11E1
Lealholm	28F3
Leamington Spa	10B5
Leasowe	20C5/24G5/45G4
Leatherhead	5C2
Ledbury	9C2
Lee	40E2
Leeds	21D3/42A3
Leicester	16F3
Leigh	5D5
Leigh on Sea	6A5
Leighton Buzzard	10D1
Lelant	1E4
Lenham	6C4
Lenzie	29B5/44D5
Leominster	9B1
Letchworth	11E2
Leuchars	34F4
Levenshulme	20C1/24G1/45A3
Levisham	22A5/28G2
Lewes	5F4
Lewisham	40E3
Leyland	20A3/24E3
Leyton	40B3
Leyton Midland Road	40B3
Leytonstone	5A4/40A2
Leytonstone High Road	40B2
Lichfield City	15E5
Lichfield Trent Valley	15E5
Lidlington	10C1
Lincoln Central	16B1/17B1
Lincoln St Marks	16B1/17B1
Lingfield	5D4
Lingwood	18F2
Linlithgow	30B4
Liphook	4D1
Liskeard	1D4
Liss	4D1
Little Kimble	10E2
Little Salkeld	27D1
Little Sutton	20D4/45F5
Littleborough	21E1
Littlehampton	5G1
Littlehaven	5E2
Littleport	11A4/17G4
Liverpool Central	20C4/24G4/45F3
Liverpool Exchange	45C3
Liverpool James Street	45F3
Liverpool Lime Street	20C4/24G4/45F3
Llanaber	13A5
Llanbadarn	13C5
Llanbedr & Pensarn	19G2
Llanberis	19E2
Llanbister Road	14D2
Llanbradach	8B4/43B3
Llandaff	8C4/43B4
Llandanwg	19G2
Llandebie	7A3/43G1
Llandecwyn	19F2
Llandeilo	13G5
Llandovery	14F5
Llandrindod Wells	14E3
Llandudno	19C3
Llandudno Junction	19D4
Llandebie	7A3/43G1
Llanellyi	7B3
Llanfair Caereinion	14B3
Llanfairfechan	19D3
Llangadog	14F5
Llangammarch Wells	14E4
Llangelynin	13B5
Llangennech	7B3
Llangynllo	14D2
Llangynwyd	7B5/43E3
Llanishen	8C4/43B4
Llanrwst & Trefiw	19E4
Llanwrda	14F5
Llanwrtyd Wells	14E4
Llwyngwril	13A5
Llwynypia	8B5/43D3
Lochailort	32B5
Locheilside	32B3
Lochgelly	30A3
Lochluichart	35C4
Lochside	29C3
Lochty	34F4
Lockerbie	26A3
Lockwood	21E2/42D5
(London)	
Blackfriars	40C5
Broad Street	5A3/40C4
Cannon Street	5B3/40C4
Charing Cross	5B3/40C5
Euston	5A3/40C5
Farringdon	40C5
Fenchurch Street	5B3/40C4
Holborn Viaduct	5B3/
Kings Cross	5A3/40C5
Liverpool Street	5A3/40C4
London Bridge	5B3/40D4
Marylebone	5A3/39C5
Moorgate	40C4
Paddington	5B3/39C5
St Pancras (ML)	5A3/40C5
Victoria	5B3/39D5
Waterloo	5B3/40D5
Waterloo (East)	40D5
London Fields	40B4
London Road, Brighton	5F3
London Road, Guildford	5C1
Long Buckby	10B3
Long Eaton	16D4
Long Marton	27E2
Long Preston	24C1
Long Stanton	11C3
Longbenton	27B5
Longcross	5B1
Longfield	5B5
Longniddry	30B1
Longport	15C3/20E1
Longton	15C3/20F1
Looe	1D4
Lostock Gralam	15A2/20D2/45C5
Lostwithiel	1D3
Loudwater	5A1/10F2
Loughborough	16E4
Loughborough Central	16E4
Loughborough Junction	40E5
Loughton	5A4/11G3
Louth	17A3/22G2
Lowdham	16C3
Lower Edmonton	5A3
Lower Sydenham	40F3
Lowestoft Central	12A1/18G1
Lowestoft North	12B1/18F1
Ludlow	9A1
Luton	11E1
Luxulyan	1D3
Lydney	8B1/9E2
Lye	9A3/15G3
Lymington Pier	4F4
Lymington Town	4F4
Lympstone	2B3
Lyndhurst Road	4E4
Lytham	20A4/24E4
Mablethorpe	17A4
Macclesfield	15A3/20D1/45A5
Machynlleth	14B5
Maddieson's Camp	6E3
Maesteg	7B5/43E3
Maghull	20B4/24F4/45F2
Maiden Newton	3F2
Maidenhead	4A1/5B1/10G2
Maidstone Barracks	6C5
Maidstone East	6C5
Maidstone West	6C5
Maldon Manor	39G2
Mallaig	32A5
Malton	22B5
Malvern Link	9C3
Manchester Oxford Road	45A3
Manchester Piccadilly	20B1/24F1/45A3
Manchester Victoria	20B1/24F1/45A3
Manea	11A3/17G3
Manningtree	12E4
Manor Park	40B2
Manor Road	20C5/24G5/45G4
Manorbier	7D2
Manors	28A1
Mansion House	40C5
March	11A3/17F3
Marden	6D5
Margate	6B1
Market Harborough	16G2
Market Rasen	17A1/22G3
Markinch	30A2/34G5
Marks Tey	12E5
Marlow	10G2
Marple	21G1
Marsden	21F1
Marske	28E3
Marston Green	15G5
Martin Mill	6D1
Maryland	40B2
Maryport	26D3
Matlock	16B5/41D1
Mauldeth Road	45A3
Maxwell Park	44E3
Maybole	29F3
Maze Hill	40D3
Meadow Well	28B5
Medstead & Four Marks	4C2
Meldreth & Melbourn	11D3
Melton Mowbray	16E2
Menheniot	1D4
Menston	21D2
Meols	20C5/24G5/45G4
Meols Cop	20A4/24E4/45F1
Meopham	5B5
Merryton	44B2